The Complete Bible Baddies

Cheats, con men, even murderers – it's surprising just how many baddies there are in the Bible.

Meet Herod, a very nasty piece of work. And Zacchaeus, a cheat and a thief. Then there's Jonah the runaway, Peter the coward, and many others.

Here, together for the first time, are the compelling and memorable stories first published in two volumes as *Bible Baddies* and *More Bible Baddies*. These tales of more than twenty dastardly Bible baddies are imaginatively retold by award-winning author Bob Hartman. Were all these villains doomed? Or could they change their wicked ways?

Bob Hartman is best known for the widely acclaimed *Lion Storyteller Bible* and the other popular books in the *Storyteller* series.

The

BOB HARTMAN

Illustrations by
Ron Tiner and Jeff Anderson

LION
CHILDREN'S

A Lion Children's Book
an imprint of
Lion Hudson plc
Mayfield House, 256 Banbury Road,
Oxford OX2 7DH, England
www.lionhudson.com
ISBN 0 7459 4934 7

First printed as individual volumes
Bible Baddies (1999)
More Bible Baddies (2001)

First edition 2005
10 9 8 7 6 5 4 3 2 1 0

A catalogue record for this book is available
from the British Library

Typeset in 11.5/14 Baskerville BT
Printed and bound in Great Britain
by Cox and Wyman Ltd, Reading

Contents

Introduction

When most people think about the Bible, it's the 'good guys' who come to mind. Noah and the ark. Daniel in the lions' den. Mary and Joseph and Jesus.

So why did I choose to write not one, but two books about Bible 'baddies', gathered here under a single cover for the first time? The reason is simple. As far as I could tell, no one had ever done it before. And it's always interesting to try something new.

But there is another reason. Ever since I was a boy, going along to Sunday school with my parents, I have been fascinated by the baddies in the Bible. After all, every story needs a villain. And the stories in the Bible feature some of the most intriguing villains of all!

Some of them – the vicious King Eglon and the ruthless granny Athaliah – are just downright evil. Others are sad and tragic, like proud Pharaoh and jealous Simon Magus. Their stories are adventures, thrillers, mysteries – as powerful and exciting as tales you will read anywhere. And I hope you will cheer when they get their comeuppance or are haunted by the evil they have set in motion.

But there are other villains who are more interesting still. Oh, they're baddies, all right –

murderers and thieves, cowards and cheats. But something happens to them (something I wouldn't dream of giving away here!) and in the end they're not baddies any more. It's a kind of mystery, I suppose – maybe the most amazing mystery of them all. It's what makes these Bible baddies so fascinating. It's what made me want to write about them. And I hope it makes you want to read about them, too!

This book is dedicated to the memory of my grandmother, who first told me the story of the evil granny I mentioned earlier. She also helped introduce me to the Mystery. Grandma's been gone a long time, but I've never forgotten her stories. I hope that the tales in this volume will be as memorable for you.

Bob Hartman

Bible Baddies

Contents

The Tyrant's Tale

▶ ▶ ▶ ▶ ▶ ▶ ▶ ▶ ▶ ▶ ▶ ▶

THE STORY OF PHARAOH

I've never liked the story of Pharaoh very much. Perhaps it has something to do with the fact that I'm the oldest of all my brothers and sisters, so that the last of the ten plagues – the killing of the first born – has always given me goosebumps. I can remember sitting in Sunday school, looking around the room and thinking, 'Yes, you would have been history, Andy Johnson. And you, too, Billy Holmes. And me too, of course!'

I was both glad that we didn't live in Egypt at the time of Moses and the Exodus, and angry that someone would put his own family at risk just to save his authority and his power. But that's what Pharaoh did. And that's how his story found its way into this book.

At first it was almost amusing.

'Did you see those two old men?' Pharaoh chuckled to

his magicians. 'They looked like a couple of goats, dragged out of the desert.'

'Desert goats!' agreed the first magician.

'Moses and A-a-a-ron,' baa-ed the second.

Pharaoh laughed out loud. 'And did you hear what they wanted?'

'LET MY PEOPLE GO!' mocked the first magician in a deep and booming voice.

'OR YOU'LL BE IN BIG TROUBLE!' boomed the second.

'THE GOD OF THE HEBREWS DEMANDS IT!' boomed Pharaoh, too. And they all laughed together.

Pharaoh wiped his eyes. 'I suppose I should cut off their heads,' he chuckled. 'But everyone needs a good laugh, now and then. And I've got to admit it: two desert tramps demanding that I, the supreme ruler of all Egypt, release some stupid Hebrew slaves is the funniest thing I've heard in a long time!'

'Ridiculous!' agreed the first magician.

'The craziest thing I ever heard!' added the second.

No one was laughing the next day, however, when Moses and Aaron walked up to Pharaoh as he strolled along the River Nile.

'Not you again!' Pharaoh sighed.

And his two magicians sighed with him.

'The Lord God has sent us,' Aaron explained. 'You refused to let his people go and so now, by his power, I will turn the waters of Egypt to blood!'

The magicians couldn't help it. They grinned, they chuckled, they burst into laughter. But when Aaron touched his staff to the river, the smiles dropped from their faces, for the water was blood-red.

'How did he do that?' Pharaoh whispered to his magicians.

'It's a… a… trick,' stuttered the first magician.

'A-anyone can do it,' explained the second.

'Then show me,' Pharaoh growled.

The magicians hurried off and managed to find a bowl of clear water. Then they walked slowly back to their master, careful not to spill a single drop. They said their secret words. They shook their sacred sticks. And the water in the bowl turned to blood, as well.

'See,' said a more confident Pharaoh to Moses and Aaron. 'Anyone can do it!'

'Anyone,' agreed the first magician, with a relieved sigh.

'Anyone at all!' proclaimed the second.

'And so,' Pharaoh concluded. 'You can tell your god that I will not let his people go.'

Seven days later, however, Moses and Aaron came to visit Pharaoh once again.

'This is starting to annoy me,' he muttered.

'And me, as well,' agreed the first magician.

'Peeved, that's what I am,' added magician number two.

But all Aaron said was, 'Frogs.'

'Frogs?' repeated a puzzled Pharaoh.

'Frogs?' echoed his two magicians.

'Frogs,' said Aaron, once again. 'Because you would not let his people go, our God will send frogs. Frogs in your houses. Frogs in your streets. Frogs all over your land.' And with that, Aaron waved his staff over the Nile and walked away.

Pharaoh glanced around. 'I don't see any frogs,' he grunted.

'No frogs here,' shrugged the first magician.

But the second magician simply said, 'Ribbit.'

'That's not funny,' Pharaoh growled.

'It wasn't me – honest,' the second magician pleaded. Then he lifted up his robe and pointed to his feet. 'It was him!'

The frog hopped slowly away. And then, all at once, an army of frogs poured out of the Nile to join him.

Pharaoh and his magicians ran as fast as they could – away from the river, away from the frogs. But when they hurried into the palace they realized there was no escape: the frogs were everywhere. Frogs on the floor, frogs on the furniture, frogs in the cups and plates and bowls!

'A simple trick,' panted the first magician.

'We can make frogs, too,' added the second.

'I'm so pleased to hear it,' Pharaoh grumbled. 'But can you make them go away?'

The magicians looked at one another, and then sadly shook their heads.

'Then fetch me Moses and Aaron,' Pharaoh sighed. 'I think it's time to give them what they want.'

So Pharaoh told Moses and Aaron that he would set the Hebrews – God's chosen people – free. Aaron smiled and raised his staff and the frogs all died.

But once they were gone, Pharaoh went back on his word and refused to let the Hebrews go.

So that is why the plagues continued, each one worse than the one before. And that is also why the magicians came to Pharaoh, at last, with a message they knew he would not want to hear.

'Your Majesty,' the first magician began, 'these plagues can only be the work of some very powerful god. You must stop the suffering. You must let the Hebrews go.'

'First there were the gnats,' moaned the second

magician. 'In our eyes and in our ears and up our noses!'

'And then there were the flies,' added the first magician. 'In our food and in our clothes and in our beds.'

'And then the animals died,' sniffled the second magician. 'The camels and the horses and the cows.'

'And now, these boils!' groaned the first magician.

'Stop your whinging!' shouted Pharaoh, as he struggled to his feet. 'Do you think that I am blind? That my family and I have not suffered as well? We, too, have swatted gnats and flies. We, too, have watched our animals die. And we, too, are now covered with these crippling sores. But if you think for a minute that I am going to give in to the Hebrews and their god, then you can think again. For I am Pharaoh, King of all Egypt, and no one – no one in heaven and no one on earth – is going to tell me what to do!'

And so the plagues continued.

Hail rained down on Pharaoh's fields and crushed all Egypt's crops. Then anything left growing was devoured by hungry locusts. Finally, darkness covered the whole of the land. And when the magicians had grown tired of bumping into the furniture and having nothing to eat, they took their empty stomachs and their skinned knees one last time into Pharaoh's palace.

They found him sitting – alone. He was no longer frustrated, no longer annoyed. No longer angry, no longer enraged. No, he just sat there, quietly brooding, with his teeth clenched tight and his knuckles white around the arm of his throne.

'What do you want?' he muttered, barely looking at his magicians.

'We want you to give up,' urged the first magician.

'Please!' begged the second. 'Please let the Hebrews go!'

'No one will think less of you,' the first magician argued. 'You have done all you could.'

'But the Hebrew god is just too strong!' added the second. 'And besides, we have heard. We have heard what the next plague will be.'

Pharaoh slowly raised his eyes and stared at his magicians. 'The death of the first-born,' he said softly. 'Your son, and your son,' he pointed. 'And mine as well.'

'Please, Your Majesty,' the first magician pleaded. 'My wife and I – we could not think of losing him!'

'We love our sons. And we know you love yours,' the second magician continued. 'And you have the power to save their lives!'

'Power?' sighed Pharaoh. 'What power? The god of the Hebrews controls the wind and the rain and the light. But I am just a king. And yet. And yet...' And here the king smiled a hard and cruel smile. 'And yet there is still one power that remains. The power to say "No".'

'But the children,' the magicians pleaded. 'The children will die!'

The king's smile turned into a hard and cruel stare. 'Sometimes,' he answered coldly, 'a leader has to harden his heart to the sufferings of his people for the sake of his people's good.'

'For his people's good,' sighed the first magician.

'Or for the sake of his own pride,' muttered the second magician.

'Out!' Pharaoh commanded. 'Get out!' he shouted again. 'And if you want to keep your heads, you will never return to this place!'

One week later, the magicians stood solemnly together and stared out over the Red Sea.

'So he let them go, after all,' the first magician sighed.

'The weeping. The wailing,' sighed the second magician in return. 'They say he tried hard to shut it out. But then his own son died – and that was too much, even for him.'

'So he let them go. And then he changed his mind – again!'

'I suppose he thought he had them trapped. Perhaps it never occurred to him that a god who could send locusts and hail and turn the Nile to blood could quite easily divide a sea, as well.'

'And so the Hebrews crossed on dry ground. And our own army? What about the soldiers sent after them?'

'Drowned. Drowned as they tried to follow. Drowned as the divided sea washed back over them.'

'So our suffering was for...'

'Nothing. Nothing at all.'

'And what about Pharaoh?' asked the first magician. 'What do you hear of him?'

The second magician shook his head. 'One of his servants told me that he has forbidden anyone in the palace to even speak about this event. And he has ordered the court historians to make no record of it whatsoever.'

'A proud man,' muttered the first magician.

'Proud to the end,' agreed the second.

And the two magicians turned away from the sea and walked sadly home.

The Avenger's Tale

• • • • • • • • • • • •

THE STORY OF EHUD AND EGLON

When I was a boy, I never tired of hearing the tale of
Eglon and Ehud. It was full of blood and violence
and gore – a long way removed from all that stuff about
gentleness and love that we usually heard at church on a
Sunday morning. But as I got older (and developed a deeper
appreciation for that love and gentleness stuff), Eglon and
Ehud became a little more troubling, along with a lot of the
other Old Testament battle stories. And that's why I chose to
include it in this collection.

I admit that I've done a lot of imagining and reading
between the lines in this retelling. And I've added a few things
you won't find in the Bible. But I have also tried to be true
to what facts the Bible does give us. Eglon is still a wicked
tyrant – an oppressor of the people of Israel. And Ehud is still

one of God's 'judges', chosen to rescue God's people in a time
of crisis – chosen to kill King Eglon. But even in the most
'just' cases, surely, killing has its repercussions. And that is
what this story is about.

Every night it was the same. For eighteen years, the same.
Ehud would wake up, suddenly, cold and sweating and
afraid. And that face, the face in the dream, would be
laughing at him all over again.

Shouting, that's how the dream began.

'The Moabites are coming! They've crossed the river
and they're heading towards the village!'

What followed next was a mad, rushing blur –
a spinning haze of colour and fear and sound. His father's
hand. His sister's screams. His mother's long black hair.
Goats and pots and tables, running and flying and falling
down.

And then, suddenly, everything would slow down again,
to half its normal speed. And that's when the man would
appear. The laughing man. The fat man. Eglon, King of
Moab.

He would climb down from his horse, every bit of his big
body wobbling. And with his soldiers all around, hacking
and slicing and killing, he would walk up to Ehud's family,
each step beating in time with the little boy's heart.

His father, Gera, would fall to his knees. His mother, as
well, with his sister in her arms. And then the big man,
laughing still, would raise his sword and plunge it first into
his father, and then through his mother and his sister, too.

Finally, the laughing man would raise his bloodied
sword and turn to Ehud, five-year-old Ehud. But before the
king could strike, there would come a sound, a call, from

somewhere off in the distance. The king would turn his head, look away for just a second, and Ehud would start to run – run between the burning buildings, run past his dying neighbours, run until the nightmare was over, run... until he awoke.

Every night, for eighteen years – that's how long the dream had haunted Ehud. But tonight, he promised himself, tonight the dream would come to an end. For today, King Eglon of Moab, the fat man, the laughing man, the man who had murdered Ehud's family, would come to an end, as well.

Ehud thanked God for his family, and particularly for his father, and the gift that his father had passed on to him. It was a gift that not even the Moabites could take away, a gift that made him the perfect candidate for the job he was about to do – the gift of a good left hand.

Most soldiers were right-handed. They wore their swords hanging from the left side of the body and reached across the body to draw them from their sheaths. That was what the enemy looked for, that was what the enemy watched – the right hand. For the slightest twitch, the smallest movement of that hand might signal that a fight was about to begin. So, a left-handed man enjoyed a certain advantage, particularly if his sword was hidden.

Ehud rubbed his eyes, rolled off his sleeping mat and reached for his sword – the special sword that he had designed just for this mission.

It was only eighteen inches long, far too short for battle, but just the right size for strapping to his thigh and hiding under his robes. And it was sharpened on both edges so he could cut in both directions. He'd wipe the smile from the fat man's face, all right – even if he had to slice it off!

He'd waited for this day for eighteen years. And for

those same eighteen years, the nation of Israel had been paying tribute to King Eglon. For the invasion which had destroyed Ehud's village had also swept across the land and resulted in Israel's surrender to Moab. And so, every year, great quantities of treasure and produce and livestock had to be delivered to the royal palace and presented to Eglon himself, as a sign of Israel's submission.

Today was the day – Tribute Day. And the man chosen to lead Israel's procession, chosen by God himself to walk right into the presence of the king, was none other than Ehud, the left-handed man, the man with the sword strapped to his thigh, the man who was finally in a position to set both himself and his people free.

Ehud thought he would be nervous, but instead he was overcome with a sense of calm and purpose. He led the procession, according to plan, out of Israel and across the Jordan river, past the stone statues of Gilgal and into the palace of the king.

He had imagined this moment for years – face to face, finally, with the man he hated most in all the world. 'What will I feel?' he had often wondered. 'Hatred? Disgust? The overwhelming urge to reach out and strike Eglon where he stands?' All those feelings, he knew, had to be overcome if the plan was to succeed. He had to be submissive, polite and reverential if he was to win the trust of this tyrant. But when Eglon at last appeared, Ehud was shocked by what he actually felt.

The king was still a big man – now far heavier than Ehud had remembered. So heavy, in fact, that his attendants had to help support his weight as he staggered toward his throne. And as for laughter, there was none at all, not even a chuckle – just a hard and constant wheeze as the man struggled to move.

Pity. That's what Ehud felt. And he couldn't believe it. Pity and the surprising sense that, somehow, he had been robbed. This was not the man he'd dreamed of – the fat man, the laughing man, the nightmare man. No, this was a sad and pathetic man, crippled by excess and by power and unable to raise a sword even if he had wanted to.

Still, Ehud reminded himself, there was the mission – the job he believed God had sent him to do. And pity or not, for the sake of his people, he would do it.

And so he bowed and he scraped and he uttered the obligatory words:

'Noble Potentate, Ruler of all you survey, Great and Mighty One.'

Then he stepped aside as, one by one, the gifts were laid before the king. Eglon, however, hardly paid attention. He nodded, almost imperceptibly, and acknowledged each part of the tribute with the slightest wave of his hand. It looked to Ehud as if he was bored with the whole affair, or just too old and tired to care.

When the formalities had finished, Ehud sent his entourage away, then turned to the king and said, 'I have a secret message for you, Your Majesty.'

For the first time, Eglon looked interested. His dull eyes showed some spark of life as they focused on Ehud.

'Silence!' the king wheezed at his attendants. 'This man has something to tell me.'

Ehud looked around, nervously. 'It's for your ears only,' he whispered. 'Perhaps if we could meet somewhere... alone?'

The king considered this, and then nodded. 'Very well,' he agreed. 'Meet me upstairs, in my roof chamber. It's cooler there, anyway. Oh,' and here he glanced at the sword that hung from Ehud's side, the long sword, the decoy

sword, 'you will, of course, leave your weapon outside.'

Ehud smiled and bowed, 'Of course!'

That smile never left Ehud's face – not once, while he waited for the king to be helped up to his chamber. For the plan was working perfectly, as all the spies had said it would. Eglon loved secrets, they had assured him. Dealing and double-dealing, they explained, was how he had hung onto his throne. And that made this plan all the more sweet. For Ehud's robe concealed a secret that the king would never expect!

Finally, the guards called Ehud up to the roof chamber. They looked at him suspiciously. They took away the sword that hung at his side. Then they sent him in to the king.

Ehud bowed again. And the king waved him forward.

'So who is this message from?' asked Eglon, and the cruelly calculating look in his eyes reminded Ehud, at last, of the man he saw each night in his dreams.

'From one of your commanders?' the king continued. 'Or from one of your spies? Or perhaps the sight of all that treasure has convinced you to speak for yourself – to betray your own people?' And with that, the king began to laugh. A little, choked and wheezing laugh, but it was enough – enough to rekindle Ehud's ebbing wrath, enough to force him to play his secret hand.

'No,' he answered firmly. 'The message is not mine nor my commanders'. The message I have for you is from God himself.' And he reached his left hand under his robe and drew his sword.

Three times – that was how he had always planned it. Once for his father, once for his mother, once for his poor murdered sister. But the first blow was so fierce, that the sword plunged all the way in, swallowed up past its hilt in the fatty folds of Eglon's stomach. And even though Ehud tried to retrieve it, all he got was a fistful of entrails and blood.

Ehud locked the chamber doors to buy himself some time, then he hurried out down the servants' staircase. A part of him wanted to savour this moment – to stand and gloat over Eglon's bloated corpse. But if he was to avoid a similar fate, he needed to run. And he thanked God for the escape route the spies had plotted out for him.

Down from the roof chamber and along the quiet corridors of the private quarters – that was the plan. And, sure enough, he passed no one but a startled maid. He rehearsed it as he went: one more turn, one more hallway, and he would be out. But as he dashed around the final corner, he stumbled over something and fell in a sprawling heap onto the floor.

It was a boy. A little boy. 'He's not hurt,' thought Ehud with relief.

'Who are you?' the little boy asked, as he picked himself up and flashed a friendly smile.

'I'm... umm... it's not important,' Ehud stammered. 'I have to be going.'

'Well, if you see my grandfather,' the boy said, 'will you tell him I'm looking for him? He said he would tell me a story.'

'Your grandfather?' asked Ehud.

'The king, silly!' the little boy grinned. 'Everybody knows that!' And Ehud just stood there, frozen.

He could hear the chamber doors crashing down. He could hear the shouts of the attendants, and their cries, 'The king, the king is dead! Someone has murdered the king!'

He had to go. He had so little time. But all he could do was stand there. And look at the boy. And look at his own bloodied hand. And look at the boy again. And watch as the smile evaporated from his innocent five-year-old face.

And then Ehud ran. Ran as he ran in his dream. Out of the palace and past the stone statues to the hills of Seirah. The army of Israel was waiting there – waiting for his return. And as soon as he shouted, 'King Eglon is dead!', the army swooped down to the valley below.

Ten thousand died that day. Moab was defeated. Israel was freed. And Ehud had his revenge, at last. And, after much carousing and shouting and celebrating, he rolled, exhausted, onto his mat, looking forward to his first full night's sleep in eighteen years.

But unlike Ehud's enemies, the dream would not be so easily defeated. For as the night wore on, it returned – more real than ever.

There was the little boy. There was the shouting. There was the slashing and the screaming and the dying… Ehud trembled and shook, just as he had done for eighteen years. But when he looked, at last, into the eyes of the man with the bloodied sword, Ehud awoke with a start. For the man with the sword was left-handed. And the killer's face was his own.

The Murderer's Tale

● ● ● ● ● ● ● ● ● ● ●

THE STORY OF DAVID

When I was a kid, I always wanted to know – who were the 'good guys', and who were the 'bad guys'? I guess that's why I found the story of David and Bathsheba so confusing. As far as I could tell, David was one of the good guys. He defeated the evil giant, Goliath. He escaped the murderous pursuit of King Saul. And he became the greatest ruler that Israel ever had.

And yet, there was that other story. The one about the naked lady on the rooftop who caught David's eye. The one we always giggled at in our Sunday school class. The one where David wasn't such a good guy after all.

What's the difference between the good guys and the bad guys? Maybe it has to do with the choices people make once they've done something wrong. Ignoring wrongdoing,

*or explaining it away, or trying to act as if it was a good thing,
seems to make them badder still. But when they admit that they
have been wrong, and give God the chance to do something
about it, he makes it possible for them to be good guys again.
Even when they've stumbled just as far as David had. Yes, even
David, the one the Bible calls, 'a man after God's own heart'.*

It was like walking down the stairs. The first step was easy,
so easy that he hardly noticed his feet had moved. He saw
her. He fancied her. He wanted her. It was as simple as that
and more complicated than his passion would allow. For he
was the King of Israel. And she was another man's wife.

There must have been some part of him willing to admit
that this was wrong. But her lips, and her skin, and her soft
falling fountain of hair covered him and consumed him and
chased away every other care. And the most he could
remember thinking was that God 'owed him one'.

He'd killed the giant, after all. And united the kingdom.
And repaid the cruelty of his predecessor, Saul, with
kindness and patience and respect.

He was David, God's chosen and anointed king. David,
faithful and trusting and true. Surely, he thought, this little
indiscretion, this passing moment of passion, could do no
long-term harm.

It was like walking down the stairs. But, suddenly, they
were narrow and steep and uneven. And the second step
proved much harder than the first.

'I'm pregnant,' explained Bathsheba. 'And there is no
question about it. The child is yours.'

Of course it was his. Her husband, Uriah, was away at
war. Fighting David's war. But there was still time to avoid

a scandal. And a way to do it, as well. It would involve a little deception, yes. But surely that was better than the humiliation of God's chosen king. So David called Uriah home from the front.

'You've fought hard!' David said. 'You've fought well!' And then, with a nod and a wink, he added, 'Spend tonight at home with your wife. It's the least you deserve.'

Uriah left the king. But he did not go home. He lay down outside the king's palace, instead, with the rest of the king's servants. So when the morning came, David sent for him again.

'I meant what I said,' he explained. 'You've had a long journey. Go home, spend some time with your wife!'

'But how can I?' Uriah sighed. 'My commander Joab and all my fellow soldiers are camping out in the fields. How could I possibly enjoy myself when I should be doing my duty and sharing in their hardship? You're a soldier too, Your Majesty. I know you understand these things. And so I shall sleep outside again tonight.'

David kept on trying. He invited Uriah to stay in Jerusalem for two more days. He fed Uriah and he flattered Uriah and he gave him so much wine to drink that Uriah could barely stagger outside each night. But still Uriah would not go home. For he was a faithful soldier, more faithful than David had ever imagined.

And that's what made the third step so hard.

It was like walking down the stairs. But now those stairs were crumbling under David's feet, and it seemed as if there was nothing he could do but fall.

A scandal had to be avoided. There was no question about it. And, more than that, Bathsheba was no longer just a passing fling.

He hadn't managed to talk Uriah into sleeping with her, but he had convinced himself completely. She was beautiful. She was carrying his child. And he wanted her. Not just for an afternoon's entertainment – but for ever. And there was only one way to make that happen. He would have to take the final step – from adultery, to deceit… to murder.

He sent the letter by Uriah's own hand.

'Give this to your commander, Joab,' he ordered. 'It is for his eyes only.'

A lesser soldier, an unfaithful servant, might have read the letter, and in so doing, saved his life. But Uriah was a good man, so he delivered his own death warrant into Joab's hand.

'Put Uriah at the front,' the letter said, 'at the spot where the fighting is hardest. Then pull your men back – and leave him alone to die.'

Joab did what he was told. He had no reason to question his king's command. David wanted this man dead. Who was he to argue?

When the news reached Bathsheba, she wept. And when the time of mourning was over – the proper time, the respectable time – David took her into his palace and married her.

It was over. It was done with. David should have been happy. But he wasn't. Because he knew that what he'd done was just like walking down the stairs. And the stairs had led him to a dungeon.

Everywhere he looked, there was darkness.

Guilt shadowed his every move. Bright days seemed cloudy. Good friends seemed distant. And even the reports of victory from the battle front seemed hollow – for they reminded him of the face of only one fallen soldier.

As for Bathsheba, was it just his imagination, or the way the evening sun caught her eye? But he couldn't help feeling that she looked different, too. Did she know? Had she guessed? And would that suspicion – if that was even what it was – for ever come between them?

And God. The God who had defeated the giant and rescued David in the desert and given him his throne. God, his light and his salvation. Even God seemed dark and distant now.

What was wrong with all of them? He had done what he had to do, and now there was no way to undo it. All he could do was put things behind him and try to carry on. So that's what David did with his guilt and his sadness and his shame. He stuffed them deep down inside himself – as he'd once stuffed supplies into a bag and taken them to his brothers, as he'd once stuffed five small stones into his hand.

The darkness, however, would not go away. The dungeon walls refused to disappear. So that's where he was sitting one day when the prophet, Nathan, came to call.

'I have a story to tell you,' Nathan announced. And David just sighed and waved for him to go on. The darkness was real. The dungeon walls were closing in. It was hard to see how a story could help.

'Make it quick,' David ordered. 'I have things… to think about.'

'Once upon a time,' Nathan began, 'there were two men. One was rich and the other poor. The rich man had more sheep than he could count, but the poor man had only one – a little ewe lamb which he cuddled and cared for and raised like one of his own children. He fed it from his table. He let it drink from his mug. No lamb was ever loved more.'

David forced a weary smile. 'If only life were as sweet

35

and simple as stories,' he thought.

'One day,' Nathan continued, 'the rich man had a visitor. He wanted to make this visitor a meal – the very best meal. But he wasn't keen to sacrifice any of his own lambs. So guess what he did? He went out and stole the poor man's lamb, and made a meal of it, instead.'

Something erupted inside David. His own guilt and anger exploded at the man in the story.

'Who is this man?' David shouted. 'Tell me his name and I promise you, he will be punished.'

The prophet looked at the king and then said very slowly, 'The man in the story... is you.'

Everything stopped for a second. It was as if David had been run through with a sword or slammed into a cold hard wall. And then, just as if he were sliding down the face of that wall, he dropped slowly to his knees.

Nathan knew. Of course, he knew. God had told him. And God had known all along.

'There will be a price to pay,' the prophet continued. 'Your family will be plagued with violence. Your wives will be unfaithful. And your child, the child that Bathsheba is carrying, will die.'

The tears came rushing out now, just as the anger had. 'I have sinned,' admitted David, at last. 'I and I alone have brought this pain upon the people I love.'

And with that admission, suddenly, there was light. It didn't make sense. There should have been darkness and more darkness still. But instead there was light. Not much light, but enough to see again, enough to make his way out of the dungeon.

And so David stood, weeping still.

'I'm sorry,' he said to Nathan.

'I'm sorry,' he said to God.

It was a small step, a feeble step, the first of many hard and painful steps. But it was a step towards the light. In fact, it was just like walking – walking back up the stairs.

The Con Man's Tale

• • • • • • • • • • • •

THE STORY OF GEHAZI

Many biblical characters lived up to the meaning of their names. Abraham became 'the father of a multitude'. Peter proved, in the end, to be a 'rock'. And Jesus was most definitely 'God's Saviour'.

Gehazi, on the other hand, managed to live down to his name. 'Belittler', 'diminisher', that's what 'Gehazi' means. And that's how he lived his life. He was a servant of the prophet Elisha and a witness to many miracles. But his response to at least one of those wonders was to reduce it to an opportunity for personal gain.

Next to the murder, oppression and betrayal you will find in the rest of this book, Gehazi's misdeeds don't seem so bad. Or, maybe it's just more common to take something beautiful and pure and turn it into something cheap and dirty and *insignificant. It's the trick of the gossip, the liar, the con man. And maybe, in the end, it's one of the most destructive kinds of badness of all.*

'That's right!' Gehazi boasted. 'I worked for Elisha: the Number One Servant to the Number One Prophet in all Israel!'

His companions shuffled closer to the fire, eager to hear what Gehazi had to say, yet careful for their numb fingers and toes. For they were lepers, every one of them.

'You must have seen some amazing things!' one leper whispered.

'Tell us about them,' begged another.

'Where does one begin?' Gehazi sighed. 'Particularly when one's stomach is complaining. I don't suppose… ?'

'Yes, yes of course!' said a third leper, handing him a piece of bread. 'Tell us your story and you can share our little meal.'

'But get on with it!' came a fourth voice, a muffled voice, from out of the darkness. 'We haven't got all night!'

'The woman from Shunem,' announced Gehazi through a mouthful of bread. 'That is where we will begin!' Then he swallowed hard and cleared his throat. 'She was rich. I can tell you that, for a start.'

'And beautiful?' asked one of the lepers.

'Not my type,' Gehazi shrugged. 'And as for Elisha? Well, who can say? What I can tell you is that every time we passed through Shunem, we visited there. Just for meals, at first, but then she talked her husband – who was much older than her, by the way – into fixing up a little room for us. A bed, a lamp, a table. All mod cons!'

'A bed!' sighed one of the lepers.

'And a table!' sighed another.

'What can I say?' Gehazi bragged. 'Elisha's an important fellow. And don't let anybody fool you – this prophet thing is not *all* about pain and sacrifice. It's also got its fair share of fringe benefits!

'So, anyway, there we were, in the lap of luxury, so to speak, when we heard something. It was the lady. The rich lady. And she was downstairs, crying.

'Well, Elisha turned to me and he said, "What do you think is the matter?"'

'Some prophet, eh? Asking *me*!' Gehazi sniggered. 'Anyway, I said the first thing that came into my head. Her husband was old. She had no children. Maybe that was the problem.

'Elisha nodded and thought about this for a minute. Then he told me to go and fetch her. Well, she stood there in the doorway, drying her eyes, and you're never going to believe what he told her.

' "A year from now..." he said, "a year from now you will be standing in that same doorway, holding a son in your arms!"

'I couldn't believe it! I mean, there we were, set up like kings: beds, tables, lamps, and three square meals a day! And he wanted to go and ruin it all! He got her hopes up. He got her all excited. But he never stopped to think – what if we showed up a year later, and there was no little boy in her arms? What then? No food to eat. No place to stay. That's what!'

And here Gehazi stopped.

'Well... what happened?' asked one of the lepers. 'Did she have the baby or not?'

Gehazi held up his hands. 'In a minute,' he gasped. 'I'm getting a little parched, here. I don't suppose there's any wine in that bag of yours?'

'Yes. Yes, of course,' said the lepers.

'And another piece of that bread would be nice,' Gehazi added.

'Well, it's all we've got, but...'

And before the leper could finish, Gehazi grabbed the bread from his hand. He swallowed the wine and he stuffed the bread in his mouth. But while he was still chewing, the man at the edge of the circle coughed.

'You were going to tell us what happened,' he said.

Gehazi nodded, chewed some more, and then after one last, large swallow, he answered. 'She had the child. Simple as that.'

'So it was a miracle!' marvelled one of the lepers.

'If you say so,' Gehazi shrugged. 'Or maybe it was just a happy coincidence. Who knows?' And then the fire caught a gleam, a nasty gleam, in Gehazi's eye.

'Or, maybe...' he suggested. 'Just maybe...' And then he stopped himself. 'No, I'd better not.'

'Tell us! Please tell us!' the lepers shouted. 'What do you think really happened?'

'We... ell...' Gehazi leaned forward and whispered, 'I have no proof of this. It's all circumstantial. But Elisha would often send me off on long errands. And that meant, of course, that he was alone with the woman in the house!'

The lepers gasped, 'You don't mean... ?'

'Anything's possible,' Gehazi grinned.

The lepers nudged and sniggered and poked at each other. They'd never heard anything like this before!

'Tell us more!' they begged.

'Yes,' came the voice from the darkness, quieter now, and more intense. 'Tell us more.'

'Well, I'll have to have another drink,' Gehazi began, as he grabbed for the wine and nearly finished it. Then he

thought for a moment and said, 'The son. Why don't I tell you about the woman's son?

'It was years later. The boy was old enough to go and help the workers in the fields. Well, one day, he started complaining about headaches. "My head! My head!" he shouted. And he wouldn't stop. So one of the servants took him home. And later that day he died.'

'The poor boy!' moaned one of the lepers.

'And the poor mother, too,' moaned another.

'Can I go on?' asked Gehazi, annoyed at the interruption. 'Now we didn't know anything about this. We were up on Mount Carmel, at the time, when Elisha saw the boy's mother galloping towards us on one of her donkeys. She was riding him for all he was worth. It was obvious that something was wrong. I mean, rich ladies don't usually go tearing around on the backs of donkeys. So Elisha sent me down to see what she wanted.

' "How are you?" I asked. "How's your husband? How's the little boy?" Well, she mumbled something about everything being fine, but I knew it wasn't, of course, because she rode right past me as if I wasn't even there and headed straight for Elisha.

'I ran after her, and it was a good thing. Because as soon as she got to the top, she jumped off the donkey and went for Elisha. I grabbed her and I pulled her away. It was lucky for him that I was there. But then – well, you know how it is with these prophets – he did the strangest thing. He told me to let go of her.

' "There's something wrong here," he said. (No kidding! I thought.) But then he admitted that God hadn't told him what it was yet.

'Well, she told him. And you didn't have to be a prophet to understand it!

' "You lied to me!" she screamed. "You deceived me! You promised me a son and now your God has taken him away!"

'Then the whole story came pouring out and, in the middle of the weeping and the wailing, Elisha handed me his staff.

' "Go to the boy!" he ordered. "Don't stop to say hello to anybody. And if anybody says hello to you, walk right past him. Go to the boy and lay my staff on his face. Now!" '

Gehazi grimaced. 'He could be pushy like that, sometimes. Anyway, I went, and even though I'm sure I offended a friend or two, I didn't stop to talk to anyone. I went straight to the house and into the child's room. And he was just lying there...'

'Dead?' asked one of the lepers.

'I guess so,' Gehazi answered. 'I mean, I'd never seen a dead person before. He could have been sleeping for all I knew. But I did what Elisha told me. I laid the staff on his face.'

'And... ? Then what?' begged another leper.

'Nothing,' said Gehazi. 'Well, what did you expect? It's not as if the staff was magical or anything. It was just a big walking stick.'

'So what did Elisha do?' asked a third leper.

'I'm getting to that,' Gehazi assured him. 'But first I think I need another drink.'

'There are only a few drops left...' one of the lepers began.

'That'll do,' said Gehazi, and then he continued.

'Elisha showed up in a little while. The boy's mother was with him. She was still pretty hysterical and she said she wouldn't leave until he did something. So Elisha went into the boy's room and shut the door.

He told me later that he prayed. Then he laid himself on

top of the boy – eye to eye, mouth to mouth, hand to hand – until the boy's skin started to get warm. Then he walked around the room for a while. Finally, he lay close to the boy again. And that's when we heard the sneeze.'

'The sneeze?' asked one of the lepers.

'Well, seven sneezes, actually. Then we knew the boy was alive.'

'Another miracle!' exclaimed the lepers.

And again Gehazi just shrugged. 'Maybe. Or maybe I was right the first time. Maybe he was just sleeping or dazed or something. And maybe the weight of the prophet started to smother him, and he choked and that's what woke him up. That would explain the sneezing for sure.'

The voice from the darkness, the muffled voice, called out again. 'So what you're saying is that this Elisha never really performed any miracles at all – that he's some kind of phoney.'

'Your words, not mine,' Gehazi grinned. And then he added, just a little nervously, 'Why don't you come closer to the fire and join us, neighbour? It's warmer here, and there's plenty to eat.'

'No, I'm comfortable where I am,' the voice called back. 'I'm afraid my features would frighten you. And, besides, it looks like you've already gobbled everything up. I was wondering, though. Could you tell us the story of Naaman? Naaman the leper.'

'A leper? Oh, yes!' everyone else chimed in.

'Naaman?' mumbled Gehazi, more nervous still. 'I don't think I remember that one.'

A coin – a single silver coin – flew out of the darkness, catching the firelight as it flipped and spun and landed at Gehazi's feet.

'Perhaps this will remind you,' the voice called out. 'And

there is another, in my bag, when you have finished.'

Gehazi's anxiety battled with his greed. And in the end, greed won – as it always did.

'Naaman?' he began. 'Well, there's not much to say. Naaman was a Syrian – a commander in their army. And he was also a leper. A little Israelite slave girl who worked in his house, told him about Elisha. So he came to the prophet, offering Elisha a small fortune, if only the prophet would heal him. Elisha passed the message on through me – yes, I remember it now – and told Naaman to dip himself seven times in the Jordan river. Naaman did what Elisha told him, and when he came up the seventh time…'

'He was healed,' the voice from the darkness finished. 'Isn't that right, Gehazi?'

'Well, yes, but…'

'But, what?' the voice continued. 'The man was a leper – more disfigured than anyone around this fire. And when he did what Elisha told him, he was healed. What could you call that, but a miracle?'

For the first time, Gehazi was speechless. So one of the lepers spoke up, instead.

'It's just a shame, isn't it, Gehazi,' he said, 'that Elisha couldn't heal your leprosy, as well.'

'Yes it is,' agreed the voice from the darkness. 'But then you haven't told us, Gehazi, how you came to be a leper in the first place.'

Gehazi wrapped his rags around himself. 'Story-time is over,' he muttered.

'No. Tell us. Tell us all,' the voice insisted, as the speaker stepped forward into the light.

'Elisha!' Gehazi gasped. And all the others gasped with him.

'Tell them, Gehazi. Tell them the truth, for once. Tell

them how I rejected Naaman's reward, because the health and the peace that the man's cure brought was reward enough. Tell them how you sneaked off and pursued Naaman. Tell them how you lied to him and told him that I had changed my mind – that I wanted some of that reward to pass out among the other prophets. Then tell them how you took that money and those expensive clothes and hid them away for yourself! Tell them how you stole that reward, Gehazi – tell these men, these poor men, whose meal you have stolen, as well.'

'But what about his leprosy?' asked one of the men.

'His leprosy is his punishment,' Elisha sighed. 'But it was always my hope that it would also be his salvation – that his disfigured body would help him to see how disfigured his heart had become. That's why I came here tonight. To search him out. To see if he had changed. But he is, sadly, just the same as he always was.

'Gehazi,' Elisha sighed again. 'My servant, Gehazi. No one has ever done a better job of living up to his name. Denier. Diminisher. Belittler. You have seen God's power and watched his love at work, yet all you can do is resent it and tear it down and explain it away.

'I had nothing to do with that boy's birth. He was a gift from God. And it was God who brought him back to life when he died. God healed Naaman, as well, and I am confident that he can heal other lepers, too. All of you, in fact...' and here he looked at Gehazi, 'if you will only turn to him and trust him.'

The others jumped up, eagerly begging to be the first. But Gehazi said nothing. He gave Elisha one last, long bitter look. And then he limped off into the darkness, alone.

The Runaway's Tale

• • • • • • • • • • • • •

THE STORY OF JONAH

There's nothing nice about the story of Jonah. I know that many people think there is – that the Big Fish makes it the perfect story for little kids. But there's much more to the story than that.

You see, it's not about disobedience, even though the prophet Jonah did disobey God when he ran away. And it's not about being rescued, either, even though Jonah is saved from the fish and the city of Nineveh escapes destruction. No, the story of Jonah is all about prejudice. That's right – good old-fashioned racism and hate. And as far as I can tell, there's nothing nice about that.

Jonah admits as much. The people of Nineveh are not like him. And he refuses to go and speak to them, not because he is afraid of what they will do to him, but because he is afraid *of what God will do for them, if they respond to his message.*

And that is why the story of Jonah ends so abruptly – not with an answer, but with a question: will Jonah lay aside his prejudices and choose to love whoever God loves? And, more importantly, will those who read his story do the same?

It didn't make any sense.

The words came to him in an instant, unexpected, as they always did. The voice was the same, unmistakable – it was God himself, the Maker of heaven and earth. But the message made no sense. No sense at all.

'Go to Nineveh, that great city, and speak my words to its people. For I have seen its wickedness.'

Jonah understood the part about wickedness. For Nineveh was the capital of Assyria. And Assyria was Israel's greatest enemy – not only because of her powerful army, which might sweep down at any time and destroy his people, but also because of her great immorality. Idol-worshippers. Pig-eaters. That's what the Assyrians were. Everything they did, and everything they believed was directly opposed to the holy Law that God had given Israel – the Law that Jonah had been taught to cherish and obey. They were Israel's arch enemies. Pagans, intent on destroying God's chosen people, the Hebrews. And yet, God had told Jonah to go and speak to them.

And that is what Jonah did not understand. That is what made no sense. For Jonah knew his prophet's job well: Speak God's word. Deliver God's message. And hope that those who received the message would listen and repent, and be granted God's mercy and blessing.

God's blessing on Nineveh? God's mercy – showered on the enemy of God's people? Even the possibility was unthinkable. And that is why Jonah ran away.

It didn't make any sense. Not really. Jonah couldn't run away from God, and he knew it. But he didn't want any part of the mission that God had set for him, either. So he decided that the simplest solution would be for him to get as far away from Nineveh as possible. Nineveh was east; so Jonah headed west.

He went to Joppa, first – on the coast. And there he booked a passage on a ship set for Tarshish, at the western end of the Great Sea.

All went well, until a storm came thundering out of nowhere.

'This doesn't make any sense!' the captain thought. Every sailor was kneeling in prayer. But the passenger was down in the hold, fast asleep, as if nothing in the world was wrong.

'Wake up!' the captain shouted, shaking Jonah until he stirred. 'What's the matter with you? The ship is about to break in two and you are down here sleeping. Get up! Pray to your god! And maybe he will save us.'

Jonah prayed. Or, at least he bowed his head. But the storm did not subside. Not even a little. So the sailors drew straws, determined to find out who was responsible for their troubles. And the short straw went to Jonah.

'Who are you? Where do you come from?' they demanded. 'And what have you done that could have brought such evil upon us?'

Jonah looked at the sailors and sighed. There wasn't an Israelite among them. They were pagans, one and all. Pig-eaters. Idol-worshippers. How could they possibly understand?

'I am a Hebrew,' he explained. 'And I worship the Lord God, the God who made the earth and sea – and everything else that is! He is the One I am running from. He is the One who is responsible for this storm.'

The sailors trembled. 'What can we do, then? Tell us – how do we appease your god? How do we stop the storm?'

'There is only one way,' said Jonah slowly. 'You must throw me into the sea.'

It didn't make any sense. The sailors should have jumped at Jonah's offer. They should have thrown him overboard and gone safely on their way. But they didn't. Instead, they took up their oars and rowed even harder for shore, hoping to outrun the storm.

'Is it possible?' Jonah wondered. 'Are these pig-eaters, these idol-worshippers, actually trying to save me?'

Whatever the intention, their efforts proved futile. For the harder they rowed, the higher the sea rose around them. Until, at last, there was no way out. Either Jonah would drown, or they *all* would!

So they fell to their knees again – and Jonah could hardly believe this – they prayed not to their own gods, but to the Lord!

'God! God of heaven and earth,' they cried, 'forgive us for what we are about to do.'

Then they tossed Jonah overboard, and immediately the sea grew calm. And as the prophet sank deeper and deeper beneath the waves, they worshipped the prophet's God and offered a sacrifice to his name.

It didn't make any sense. Somehow, Jonah was still alive! He could hear himself breathing. He could feel his heart beating. And the smell – phew! – he had never smelt anything so awful in his life! But when he opened his eyes, everything was dark.

He shook his head and tried to remember. He remembered the crashing waves. He remembered struggling

for the surface and saving each tiny bit of breath. And then, just before he passed out... he remembered! The fish! The biggest fish he had ever seen! And it was swimming straight for him.

'Is it possible?' Jonah wondered. 'It must be. It has to be! I am sitting in the belly of that fish!'

And, no, it still didn't make any sense. Jonah had disobeyed God. He knew he deserved to die. And yet God had preserved him and sent this fish – he was sure of it! And that meant, surely it meant, that God still had work for him to do, and that he would see the light of day, once more!

And so Jonah prayed a prayer. Not a prayer for help, but a prayer of thanksgiving, as if the help had already come. As if the belly of this fish were a temple, and he was seated in the midst of it – ribs standing tall like pillars, the odour of entrails rising like incense to Jonah's God.

> 'I was in danger. So I cried to God.
> I cried to him and he answered me.
> From the belly of hell I cried
> And the Lord God heard my voice!
>
> It was he who cast me in the sea,
> Far beneath the crashing waves,
> With the waters roaring round me,
> And the surface like the sky.
>
> And so I thought
> That I had been banished,
> Cut off from God
> And his temple for ever.

'Down I went,
Down deeper and deeper,
Down to the feet of the mountains,
Seaweed wrapped around my head.

Down, still further down,
Down, and no escape.
And that is when you reached me
And rescued me from the watery pit.

Idol-worshippers don't understand.
Their requests count for nothing.
But I will give you thanks,
Offer sacrifices in your name,
For you are my great deliverer!'

Three days and three nights. That's how long Jonah waited in the belly of the fish. Then it belched him up onto dry land, and those words came pouring into his head again: 'Go to Nineveh, that great city, and tell them that I have seen their wickedness.'

It still didn't make any sense. Not to Jonah. But he wasn't about to argue, this time. So he travelled east, all the way to Nineveh. And when he got there, his mission made less sense than ever!

'This city is enormous!' sighed Jonah. 'It will take me days just to walk across it. How can my message possibly make any difference?'

But Jonah was determined not to end up in another fish's belly. So he started to preach.

'Forty days!' he said to anyone who would listen. 'Forty days to change your ways. Or else God is going to destroy your city.'

'This is useless!' Jonah sighed. 'These pig-eaters, these idol-worshippers, are never going to change.'

However, day after day, he preached. And day by day, the people of Nineveh began to take notice. There were just a few, at first, but soon the whole city was on its knees – from the humblest servant to the king himself – weeping and praying and asking God's forgiveness.

'This doesn't make any sense!' Jonah grumbled.

'No sense at all!' Jonah groused. 'You had the perfect opportunity, God, to destroy your enemy, and the enemy of your people. But you let it pass, and now – look at them – pig-eaters and idol-worshippers, praying, confessing, repenting and asking for forgiveness!

'Can you see, now, why I ran away? This won't last. They'll be up to their old tricks again in no time – you'll see! And then they'll be out to destroy us all over again.'

And at that moment, Jonah had an idea.

'I'll get out of the city,' he thought. 'I'll get out of the city and sit on the hillside and watch. Watch and wait for them to turn from God again. And then, maybe then – God will destroy the Ninevites once and for all!'

But his thoughts were interrupted by a voice.

'Jonah,' God called.

'Jonah!' God summoned. 'Do you really think it's right for you to be angry with me?'

But Jonah paid God no attention. He was too busy building a little shelter and stocking it with provisions, so that he could sit and watch the city's ruin.

So God got Jonah's attention another way. He made a tree grow up over Jonah's shelter, to shade him in the heat of the day. But just as Jonah had started to appreciate the shade, God sent a worm in the night to kill the little tree.

'This doesn't make any sense!' Jonah moaned. 'This tree was here one day, and gone the next. Now I'll have to sit and sweat.

'Life is so unfair!' he complained. 'I wish I was dead!'

And that's when the voice, the unmistakable voice, the voice of God himself, came pouring, once again, into Jonah's head.

'I'll tell you what makes no sense, Jonah,' the voice began. 'You grieve at the death of this tree, but you have no concern whatsoever for the people – the thousands of people – who live in the city below.

'Yes, they are idol-worshippers, as far from understanding me as a young child is from knowing its right or left hand. But I love them. And I have forgiven them. And if my ways are ever going to make any sense to you, Jonah, then you will have to lay aside your prejudices and learn to love them, too.'

The Heartless King's Tale

THE STORY OF HEROD

What do you think of when someone says 'Christmas'? Stars and angels, right? Giving and peace and goodwill! The story of the first Christmas is filled with those images. But, like most stories, it has a villain, too. A selfish and cruel villain who does everything he can to rob the story of its wonder. A villain with a dark story all of his own.

I thought it would be interesting to set the story of Christmas and Herod's story side by side – the story of Herod and that of the child he tried to kill. Not only because the stories are so different, but also because the difference offers a vivid illustration of the contrast between good and evil – between God's gift of life and one man's deadly ambition.

The night was crisp and clear. The stars shone bright like candles. A mother cradled a child in her arms. And when she closed her eyes and listened, she could almost hear the angels sing.

The old man in the palace, however, wasn't interested in angels. Ghosts were his companions. And they followed him, now, wherever he went.

It hadn't always been this way. When he was young, there was just too much to do. A kingdom to win. Power to establish. And enemies, more than he could count, to be dealt with and disposed of. And even when the bodies piled up – like stones stacked for his brand new temple – the ghosts stayed respectfully still.

How could he have known that they were just waiting – waiting for him to grow old and sick, waiting for him to grow tired, waiting for long and lonely winter nights.

The ghost of his uncle.

The ghost of his aunt.

The ghost of his wife.

The ghosts of his ambitious sons.

Murdered, each and every one. Murdered at his command. Murdered because they tried to take his throne.

'I am the King of the Jews!' he growled. Growled at the darkness. Growled at the walls. Growled at the noisy company of ghosts.

'I am the King of the Jews!' he growled again. 'Herod. Herod the Great!'

The walls did not answer. The darkness stayed silent and deep. But a knock at the door startled the king and sent him shaking.

'Who is it?' he whispered. 'What is it?' he called. And his heart slowed to a steady beat only when a servant stuck his head into the room.

'Visitors, Your Majesty,' the servant answered.

'At this hour?' the king shouted. 'Tell them to go away!'

'But they say it is urgent, Your Majesty. They have travelled, day and night, all the way from Babylon, following a star! A star which, they say, will lead them to our newborn king.'

Herod's heart started racing again. First the ghosts, and now this. Would he never be able to rest? And so, wearily he sighed, 'Send them in!'

The night was still and peaceful. The angels kept their silent watch. The carpenter kissed the baby and told his wife how he loved her.

But in the palace of the king, everyone was stirring.

'So you're looking for a king?' Herod asked his visitors.

'Yes,' one of them answered. 'The newborn King of the Jews.'

Herod wanted to say it. He really wanted to tell them, 'I am the King of the Jews!' But he had to control himself, he knew it, if he was to discover what these foreigners were up to.

'We have followed a star,' explained another visitor, 'all the way from Babylon. It led us here, to Judaea, and we thought you, of all people, might be able to tell us exactly where to find this new king.'

'And *why* would you want to find him?' asked Herod suspiciously.

'Why, so we could honour him with the gifts we have brought,' the visitor answered.

'So could you tell us, please?' added a third visitor. 'Even a hint would help – a prophecy, perhaps, from one of your holy books.'

'Stars and prophecies,' thought Herod. 'Stars and prophecies and ghosts. Why won't they leave me alone?' And for an instant, he considered sending these star-gazers away. But, what if... ? What if there really was a king, a baby king, out there? A king who would one day wrest the throne from him. Then he needed to know about it. He needed to find it. And he needed, most of all, to destroy it – before it had the chance to destroy him!

And so Herod shouted, 'Fetch the priests! No, the CHIEF priests! And the scribes, as well. Fetch anyone who can help us find this king!'

The night was a dark blue blanket. It lay over the hills and the shepherds and their sheep. And over the carpenter and his family, as they prepared at last to go to sleep.

But in the palace of the king, everyone was awake. Wide awake!

Herod snapped his fingers. 'Hurry!' he commanded. 'You are the experts in these things, so tell me: where do the prophets say the King of the Jews will be born?'

'Well, if it's the Messiah you mean,' answered one of the priests, 'then the prophets are very clear.'

'Bethlehem,' replied another priest, 'according to the words of the prophet Micah.'

'Excellent!' Herod smiled. 'Now you may go.'

'But if I may,' asked one of the chief priests, 'why is Your Majesty suddenly interested in this?'

'I have my reasons,' growled the king. 'Now, as I said, you may go.' And the priests hurried off into the night.

As soon as the priests had gone, Herod sent for the visitors. 'Tell me again,' he said. 'You have been following this star for how long?'

'Two years, Your Majesty,' answered one of the visitors.

Herod nodded his head. 'And so that would make this new king how old?'

'No more than two years,' the visitors explained.

'I see,' Herod nodded again. 'Well I have good news for you. My priests tell me that Bethlehem is the town you're looking for. It's not far from here.' And then, trying hard to look as innocent as possible, he added, 'Perhaps you could do me a favour? I, too, would like to honour this new king. So when you have found him, could you come and tell me exactly where he is?'

The night was bright with stars. But one star shone brightest of all. It hovered above the house of the carpenter and his family. It waited for the star-gazers, just as it had shown them the way. And then it watched as they knocked on the door, and were greeted by the sleepy carpenter, and went in to worship the child. And when they had offered their gifts and walked out of the house again, it winked goodbye and joined its brothers in the sky.

In Herod's palace, however, the king sat alone. Alone with his suspicions and fears. Alone with the ghosts.

'Yes, yes,' he muttered. 'I know what you're thinking. To make a ghost of a child is the greatest evil of all. But I can't take the chance, don't you see? No, I'm not worried about him growing up and taking my place. I'll have joined your company by then. What worries me is what might happen here and now. What if he has some legitimate claim to the throne? Or what if – God forbid! – he really is the Messiah? All my enemies would need to do is get hold of that child and use him against me. Moan all you want. Rustle the tapestries. Wail through the walls. Do what you will to frighten me. But I will not be moved from my course. When the star-gazers return, the child will die. And then he will be yours to deal with.'

The night crept over the star-gazers and swallowed them in sleep. They dreamed of shiny things – of stars and gold and bright perfume bottles. And then, something brighter still invaded their dreams – something shinier than their guiding star, purer than their golden gifts, and sweeter-smelling than all their balms and ointments. And they knew it could only be a messenger from God.

'Do not return to Herod,' the messenger warned them. 'For he is a wicked man, and he means to kill the boy. Sneak out of this country. Take another route home. And take the secret of the child with you.'

The star-gazers left at once. But Herod awoke with a start – roused by darker spirits, perhaps – and called for his guard.

'There is something wrong,' he said. 'Go to Bethlehem immediately, and bring me the visitors from the east.'

When the soldiers returned with news that the visitors had gone, Herod was not surprised. And he was not worried, either. For he had already devised a cruel alternative. So cruel that the soldiers, themselves, could hardly keep from weeping.

'You will kill every boy in Bethlehem!' he ordered. 'Every boy two years old or younger. You will be quick. You will be thorough. And you will show no mercy. This child will not escape me!'

As soon as the soldiers departed, the ghosts surrounded Herod. They clawed at his mind and tore at his heart. They raced around inside his head. And even as their numbers grew – child by murdered child – he would not be moved. Instead, he answered their dying screams with madman cries of his own: 'I am the King of the Jews! I am Herod the Great! And no one will take my throne from me!'

But as those cries echoed around his dark and ghostly bedchamber, the angels went to work again – warning the carpenter and his family and guarding them as they crept off safely and escaped into the night.

The Greedy Taxman's Tale

• • • • • • • • • • • •

THE STORY OF ZACCHAEUS

Nobody likes to pay taxes. But when the taxes go to an oppressive occupying government, and when the tax collector charges far more than he should just to line his own pocket, then it makes paying taxes that much harder to bear.

That's how it was, in Palestine, where Jesus lived. The Jewish people were ruled by the Romans, who had conquered them many years earlier. And their taxes enriched not only their conquerors, but also local tax collectors – fellow Jews who profited by collaborating with the Romans.

So tax collectors were the 'bad guys'. And you can understand why they were hated and despised and lumped, by

polite society, with the lowest of the low. But Jesus didn't look
at it that way. He spent a lot of his time with folk who were
considered 'bad', and he received his share of criticism for that.
Yet he kept on doing it all the same, because he believed that no
one was out of reach of God's forgiveness and life-changing
love. Not even greedy tax collectors – like Zacchaeus.

He loved the sound of coins.

The ringing and the jingling as they rained out of his cupped hand.

The clicking and the clacking as they struck the wooden table.

And the soft 'shoop-shoop' as he slid each one into its pile.

He loved the sound of coins. So there was no better time than counting time. And his servants had strict instructions that he was to be left alone, in peace and in quiet – instructions that they were more than willing to keep, for he was a hard and a miserable master, even at the best of times.

Drop a cup, or rattle a pot, or – heaven forbid! – break a bowl or a pitcher, and an angry 'QUIET!' would echo from the counting room. And so his servants tiptoed around the house at this time of day, terrified of making even the slightest noise.

Their fear and their anxiety meant nothing to him, however. His servants were, after all, no more than coins as far as he was concerned.

Five coins for the cook.

Two for the maid.

And one for the boy who minded his donkey.

And names? What was the point of learning names? They never stayed that long. And anyway, it was the coins, the coins that counted.

The coins he took from the citizens of Jericho.

The coins he passed on to the Roman Government.

And, most important of all, the coins he kept for himself!

That was the sum total of the tax collector's life. As for multiplying friendships, well, that was simply not prudent. For friends would only use the relationship to wriggle out of their obligation. And adding acquaintances? That was no more likely. For what time was left when the collecting and the counting was done? And who would want to be seen with a Roman collaborator, anyway?

No. Taking away the hard-earned money of Jericho, and dividing the piles between himself and the Romans – that was what mattered. And the coins. The sound of counting coins.

But, one day, there came another sound. A sound he couldn't ignore. The sound of laughter and cheering and crowds. And the tax collector was quick to react.

'Quiet!' he shouted. But the sound did not go away.

'Quiet, I said!' he shouted more loudly. And still the sound would not cease.

'QUIET!' he shouted a third time, as loudly as he could, banging his fist on the table and sending a tingling quiver through the coins. 'QUIET! I NEED QUIET!'

At last, the door creaked open, and a frightened whisper crept into the counting room. 'We're very sorry, master, but there is nothing we can do about the noise. It's coming from the street.'

'Then clear the rabble away!' the taxman growled. 'I have work to do. I need quiet.'

'But sir,' the voice pleaded, 'it's not just a few people. Everyone is out there. Everyone in Jericho!'

'Another holiday, I suppose,' groaned the tax collector. Then he launched into a tirade that the servant had heard a hundred times before.

'These people – they complain about paying their taxes. "It's a day's wage!" they moan. "How will we feed our families?" But give them a holiday, and they'll gladly lose a day's wage – the hypocrites!'

'But it's not a holiday, sir,' the servant answered. 'It's Jesus. The teacher and miracle-worker. Jesus has come to town!'

The tax collector groaned again. If there was one thing he hated more than noise, it was religion. It wasn't just the long list of rules – the dos and don'ts that would put any self-respecting taxman out of business. No, it was the money.

A coin for the priest.

A coin for the temple.

A coin for the sacrifice.

A coin for the poor.

And soon there were no coins left!

Again, he just couldn't understand the hypocrisy. The people hated him for what he took, but they were glad to give up a tenth of what they earned – and more! – so that priests, who were already fatter than him, could grow fatter still.

'I have no time for religion!' the taxman shouted. 'I have work to do!'

'Ah, but Jesus is different,' said the servant, thinking fast and hoping to win a little favour. 'They say he's the friend of tax collectors!'

'The friend of tax collectors?' sneered the taxman. 'That'll be the day!' And he slammed the door shut, nearly smashing his servant's nose.

And yet... as he sat there and counted, the taxman's curiosity grew.

'A religious teacher *and* the friend of tax collectors?' he wondered. 'How exactly does that work?' And then the tax collector grinned. For the first time in a long time, a mischievous smile found its way onto his face.

'Blessed are the shaker-downers,' he chuckled. 'And the rougher-uppers, and the over-chargers, and the bottom-liners. Blessed are the tax collectors!' he cheered. And at that moment, he made up his mind. He would leave his counting for the moment. He would venture out into the street. He would go to see this Jesus!

Now don't be mistaken. This was not a rash decision. As with everything else in his life, he counted the cost carefully. If he was spotted, he would certainly be cursed or spat upon or possibly even attacked by some angry taxpayer he'd overcharged or by some political fanatic who resented his connections with the Roman overlords. But a quick peep out of the window assured him that everyone's attention was turned to the street. So who would notice if someone – particularly someone small of stature like himself – were to sneak quietly behind the crowd and have a look?

And that's just what the tax collector did. He locked up his coins and he crept out the door and he picked his way carefully along the back of the crowd. But it wasn't long before he realized that there was one part of the equation he had not taken into account: Smallness was good for sneaking. Smallness was good for creeping. Smallness was especially good for not being seen. But as far as *seeing* was concerned, smallness was no good at all!

Yes, he could have wriggled and squirmed his way through the crowd. But that would have been unwise. For there, in that gap, was the broad backside of Benjamin the butcher, who had threatened him with a very sharp knife last time the taxes were due. And in the next gap were the unmistakably flat feet of shepherd Baruch – feet that had found their way to the tax collector's bottom a time or two. And over there? Well, what did it matter? The crowd was packed with people he had deceived or cheated or overcharged.

And then he saw it, standing tall at the end of the street. A single sycamore tree, with branches broad enough and full enough to conceal a small and nervous tax collector. And just high enough to give him a perfect view.

So over he crept and up he climbed, and because the crowd was so keen to see Jesus, no one noticed him. No one at all.

The tax collector, however, could see everything. There was Jesus, or at least that's who he assumed it was, greeting the cheering crowd. And there were the town dignitaries, of course, the rich and respected ones, pushing their way to the front. He knew what they were saying, even though he was too far away to hear:

'Come to *my* house, Jesus!'

'Eat at *my* table, Jesus!'

'Visit *my* home, Jesus!'

There was nothing hospitable about this, of course. Each and every one of those hypocrites was just anxious to hear the 'Ooohs' and 'Aaahs' of the crowd when this famous holy man agreed to honour their house with his presence.

But as the tax collector watched, the most remarkable thing began to happen. With every greeting, with every request, Jesus gently shook his head – 'No thank you.'

'Is he leaving town so quickly?' the tax collector wondered. 'Or has he already made some other arrangements? If not, he had better make up his mind soon, for he's almost at the end of the street.'

And, at that very moment, Jesus stopped. And looked up. And spoke one word and one word only.

'Zacchaeus.'

The tax collector hardly knew what to do. He thought

he was hidden. He thought he was safe. And besides, it had been so long since he'd heard his name spoken, it hardly seemed as if it belonged to him at all. The servants called him 'sir', and the townspeople had their own selection of names. And as for anybody else. Well, there wasn't anybody else. Not until now, anyway.

'Zacchaeus!' Jesus called again. 'Zacchaeus, come down!'

And with that the crowd began to mock and to point and to howl. 'The tax collector! Look! The tax collector is up in the tree!' But their laughter collapsed into stunned silence at Jesus' next words.

'Zacchaeus,' he said again, 'I'm coming to *your* house, today.'

Leaves. Leaves against leaves – that was the only sound, as Zacchaeus climbed slowly down the tree. But with each branch, a new thought went racing through his head:

'Why is Jesus doing this?'

'Is this some kind of trick?'

'What will the people do?' and

'Is there anything in the pantry?'

It had been ages since anyone had visited his home, so Zacchaeus simply muttered, 'Come this way,' and hoped that he could remember what to do. As for the crowd, their surprise soon turned into something uglier.

'He's a thief! He's a cheat! He's a sinner!' the crowd complained. 'Why is Jesus eating with him?' Part of it was jealousy. And part of it was confusion. Holy men ate with good people – that's what they were used to. But this was different. And in that difference lay the explanation for what happened next.

Maybe it had to do with what Jesus said. Or maybe with what he did. Or maybe it was no more than Jesus' willingness to call Zacchaeus by name and offer to be his friend. But when dinner was over, Zacchaeus came out of his house again, not creeping, not sneaking, but standing tall (or at least as tall as he was able!).

'I have something to say to you,' he announced to the crowd. 'Something to say to you all. I'm sorry. I'm sorry for cheating you and deceiving you and making myself rich at your expense.' And then he waved his hand and his servants came out of the house as well, carrying bags of coins.

'My life was all about taking away. But from now on, that will be different. Half of all I own, I will give to the poor. And whatever I have stolen from anyone, I will multiply by four and return to them, here and now.'

Someone gasped. Someone shouted. And soon the whole crowd cheered.

'Salvation has come to this house!' cheered Jesus along with them. But as Zacchaeus tore open the moneybags and his fortune spilled out through his fingers, all he could hear were the coins, the sound of the coins, ringing and jingling, and somehow more beautiful than ever – now that he was giving them away!

The Politician's Tale

● ● ● ● ● ● ● ● ● ● ● ●

THE STORY OF PILATE

Sometimes, it's hard to know exactly what a biblical character was like. You piece together the information as best you can, but you're still not sure you've captured the person.

Take Pilate, for example – the Roman governor who presided over the trial and execution of Jesus. Some people have seen him as a basically good man who got caught in a difficult situation. Others have pictured him as weak and indecisive. Personally, I think the clue to his character lies in something he said to Jesus.

'I have come to tell the truth,' Jesus explained, during his trial. And all Pilate could say in return was, 'What is truth?'

You see, there are some people who try hard to live by what they believe is true. And there are others that fail to do *that. But the really scary people are the ones who don't believe that there is any truth, any right or wrong, at all. I think that's the kind of person Pilate was. And even though you may find him charming and amusing, his disregard for any truth beyond himself may well make him the baddest baddy of them all.*

Pilate rubbed his hands together and smiled at his new assistant. 'Well then, are we ready to get to work?'

Marcus smiled politely in return and nodded, 'Yes, Governor. And may I say what a pleasure it is to be working for someone who truly seems to enjoy his job.'

Pilate winked and gave the young man a knowing look. 'Excellent!' he grinned. 'Butter up the boss on your very first day. Someone's taught you well, my boy.'

'No, I meant it, sir,' Marcus responded. 'Some of my past employers just seemed to be putting in their time – waiting for that next holiday or the retirement villa by the sea.'

'Ah yes,' Pilate nodded. 'I know the type. I've worked for a few myself. But I can assure you that things are different here. I like what I do! It's difficult, sometimes. And it's always risky. But for my money, it's still the best game in town!'

'Game, sir?' asked Marcus.

'What else would you call it?' said Pilate, dropping down into his chair. 'Keep the peace. Keep the revenues rolling in. Keep Caesar happy. Those are the official rules.'

'And the object of the game, as well,' Marcus added.

Pilate chuckled. 'No, my boy. The object of the game is for "yours truly" to keep his job. And, with any luck, to keep climbing up that empire-sized ladder.'

Marcus looked a bit confused, now. 'But, sir? What about

duty? What about justice? What about right and wrong?'

Pilate's chuckle grew into a laugh. 'You do have a lot to learn, don't you?' Then he stood up on his chair and stuck his arms straight out from his sides. 'I've always thought it was a bit like walking on an aqueduct.'

'An aqueduct, sir?'

Pilate peered down at his assistant. 'You mean to tell me that you've never walked on an aqueduct? Why, when I was a boy, growing up in the Roman countryside, there was nothing I enjoyed better. My friends and I would climb up on top of the tallest one we could find. The water would be rushing down the middle, faster than any river. But along the stonework at the edge, there was just enough room to walk.'

'But wasn't that dangerous, sir?'

'Of course it was dangerous! That was the point! Fall off one side and you'd smash your head on the ground below. Fall off the other side, and the water would carry you halfway to Sicily before they could fish you out. But if you held your arms out just right – leaning a little this way and a little that way and watching carefully for which way the wind was blowing – then you could do it, and not get killed.

'That's what it's like being the governor of Palestine. A little justice here. A little oppression there. A touch of mercy. A hint of brutality. It's all the same really – just so long as you keep your balance. Just so long as you don't fall off.'

'And you enjoy that, sir?'

'More than anything, my boy,' Pilate grinned. Then he hopped onto the floor and plopped back into his chair. 'Every day is different. Every day, an adventure. So let's see what today brings. Secretary!' he called. 'Send in the first appointment.'

A short, round, bald-headed man stuck his head into the room.

'I'm terribly sorry, Governor,' he apologized, 'but I'm afraid you're going to have to come into the courtyard for this one. It's another one of their holy days, and they say they'll be defiled if they come into the building.'

'Yes, yes,' Pilate sighed. 'I know the drill.'

But the look on Marcus' face suggested that he did not.

'Defiled, sir?' he asked.

'It's a religious thing,' Pilate explained. 'The Jews are obsessed with this notion that they are God's special people. Which, of course, makes the rest of us somewhat less-than-special. So they are forbidden to have any close contact with us – to come into our homes, for example – in case it makes them unfit to participate in their religious rituals. That's the gist, anyway.'

'So what do we do?' Marcus asked.

'We humour them,' Pilate answered, sticking out his arms again and tippy-toeing forward. 'It's all about balance, remember? Our little walk into the courtyard will make the Jewish leaders happy. And, I don't know about you, but I could use the exercise!' And then Pilate chuckled. 'As they say, when in Jerusalem…'

'But what do you think they want, sir?' Marcus asked.

'Publius?' Pilate inquired, turning to his secretary.

And the secretary just rolled his eyes. 'It's another Messiah, Governor.'

Pilate clapped his hands together happily. 'Excellent! Did you hear that, Marcus? Another Messiah! We should be finished by lunch!'

'A Messiah, sir?' Marcus asked. 'I'm afraid…'

'Yes, of course. You're new.' And then Pilate stopped for a moment. 'The Messiah is a Jewish legend. The Christ. The

Anointed One. The King of the Jews. It's all the same, and it all has to do with their belief that, one day, their god will send a powerful leader to set them free from their enemies.'

'Their enemies?' asked Marcus. 'And that would be… ?'

'Us! Yes, that's right,' Pilate grinned. 'And I take it as a sign of our efficiency as conquers and overlords that so many of these Messiahs have been popping up recently. I suppose we've dealt with – what? – one a month?'

'At least, sir,' moaned Publius. 'A nuisance, if you ask me, sir.'

'Yes, well, you have to deal with the paperwork, don't you? I, on the other hand, only have to deal with the Messiahs. And frankly, I find them quite fun!'

'Fun, sir?' asked Publius and Marcus, together.

'Of course! Messiahs come in two basic shapes, you see. The hairy, under-nourished, wide-eyed, fanatically-religious shape. And the don't-turn-your-back-on-me-or-I'll-stick-a-knife-in-your-neck political revolutionary shape.

'Now the first kind is no trouble at all. You listen to them rant and rave for a few minutes, and then send them off to be flogged.

'As for your revolutionary types… well, it's the rules of the game, isn't it? Young Marcus…'

Marcus thought hard. 'Umm… Keep the peace. Keep the revenues rolling in… Keep Caesar happy!'

'Excellent! And because your basic revolutionary Messiah is all for starting trouble and disrupting trade and booting poor Caesar out of the country, what do you do? You crucify him. Simple as that!

'And so,' Pilate concluded, grinning that grin and rubbing his hands together again, 'let's see what kind of Messiah we have today!'

As Pilate entered the courtyard, he glanced at the

prisoner. The man stood quiet and still. His hair was matted, his eyes tired. It looked as if someone had beaten him up.

Next, he glanced at the crowd, then turned to his assistant and whispered, 'All the big shots are here – the Jewish leaders and their council. I'm guessing that we've got your basic religious type Messiah to deal with.'

Finally, he turned to the crowd itself. 'So tell me. What is this man charged with?'

The accusations shot forth, more fiercely than Pilate had ever heard them before.

'He stirs up the nation!'

'He tells us not to pay our taxes!'

'He says he is Christ – the King!'

'It seems like he's broken all the rules of the game,' observed Marcus.

Pilate just nodded. 'So you want me to put him to death? Is that it?' Pilate said to the crowd. 'Well, let me talk with him, first. It's Roman law that needs to be satisfied here.'

'And it will keep them in their place!' he whispered to Marcus.

Pilate took the prisoner aside and looked him straight in his swollen and bloodshot eyes.

'So you're the King of the Jews then, are you?'

'That's what they say,' shrugged the prisoner.

'Look,' Pilate answered, 'I don't care what *they* say. What I need to know is what *you* say. Are you the King of the Jews or not?'

The prisoner sighed, as if he were tired – not from lack of sleep, but for lack of being understood.

'I have a kingdom, yes. But it's not the kind of kingdom you're thinking of. If it were, my followers would be here, fighting for me.'

Now it was Pilate's turn to sigh. 'So let me get this straight,' he continued. 'You say you *are* a king, then?'

'*You* say that I am a king. But I was sent into this world for a different reason. I was sent to speak the *truth*.'

'Truth?' chuckled Pilate. 'TRUTH? What is truth?' Then he shook his head and walked back to his aide.

'Well?' asked Marcus.

'Well, he's not political – that's for sure. And he doesn't strike me as your typical fanatic, either. He's different, I'll grant you that. But he doesn't deserve to die.'

And that's what Pilate told the crowd: 'I find no crime, here. No crime at all.'

But if Pilate thought that would satisfy them, then he was wrong. They started shouting again – louder even than the first time.

'But he's stirring up the people! It started up in Galilee, and now it's spread all the way down here to Judaea.'

'They obviously hate this man,' Pilate whispered to Marcus. 'And they're not going to go away until I do something...' And then Pilate grinned and snapped his fingers.

'Did you say he's from Galilee?' Pilate shouted to the crowd. 'Well, that's not under my control. Herod Antipas is in charge of Galilee, and as it happens, he's here, in town, for your Passover festival. Why don't you take the prisoner to Herod and let him decide what to do?'

The crowd grunted and moaned. But they were eager to have their way, so they grabbed the prisoner and dragged him off to see Herod.

'There's another lesson for you,' Pilate beamed. 'When you're having trouble making a decision – or when a decision is likely to make trouble for you – pass the responsibility on to someone else!'

Pilate escorted Marcus back into his office, but it wasn't long before Publius stuck his head into the room again.

'It's that Messiah, Governor. I'm afraid he's back.'

'But what about Herod?' Pilate asked.

'It seems he's learned that lesson about passing on difficult cases, too.'

'Then he's a smarter man than I've given him credit for,' Pilate noted. 'I'll have to invite him over sometime.' Then he marched out into the courtyard, looking as 'official' as possible.

'I have already made my decision,' he announced to the crowd. 'This man has committed no crime!'

But the crowd would not be pacified, and they shouted even more loudly.

'All right! All right!' Pilate announced, 'How about this? Every year, during your festival, I release a prisoner, as a gesture of goodwill towards the community. Why don't I let this man go?'

'No!' shouted one of the priests. 'Free Barabbas, instead!'

'Barabbas?' asked Marcus.

'A thief and a murderer,' explained Pilate. 'And also something of a local hero.'

And that is why the crowd began to chant, 'We want Barabbas! We want Barabbas! We want Barabbas!'

'Ah well,' sighed Pilate, 'I hate to do it, but it's the rules of the game... All right, then,' he announced to the crowd. 'I shall set Barabbas free!' And then he pointed to the prisoner, 'But what shall I do with this man?'

'Crucify him!' the crowd chanted. 'Crucify him!'

'But he's done nothing wrong!' Pilate called back.

'He's made himself a king!' someone shouted. 'And that makes him an enemy of the true king – Caesar!'

'Yes!' shouted someone else, 'So if you set him free, then that makes you Caesar's enemy, too!'

'The hypocrites!' Pilate muttered to Marcus. 'They hate Caesar, maybe even more than they hate this man. But it's obvious. They're willing to say anything that will get him crucified. And frankly, I can't afford to let this crowd get any further out of hand. And so I suppose that it comes down to the rules of the game, once again.'

'Even if you have to execute an innocent man?' asked Marcus.

Pilate smiled. 'Well, I've thought of a way round that, as well. Publius, fill me a basin of water. And bring me a clean towel.'

'Do you see this?' called Pilate to the crowd. 'I am innocent of this man's blood!' Then he plunged his hands into the water, and ordered his soldiers to beat the prisoner and take him off to be crucified.

'Nice touch, don't you think?' remarked Pilate, once the crowd had gone. 'If I've made the right decision, then I'm the hero. And if I've made the wrong one, well, I think I'm covered there, as well.'

Marcus was not convinced. 'But don't you worry that it makes you seem weak and indecisive?'

'Not if I keep my balance!' smiled Pilate, sticking out his arms again. 'Now let's get back to work.'

The rest of the day was uneventful.

Some of the Jewish leaders complained about the sign that had been nailed on the prisoner's cross. Someone else came by to claim the man's body once he'd died. And, somewhere in the middle of the afternoon, the weather suddenly turned worse than anyone could remember.

'Well, what do you say, Marcus?' asked Pilate, as they

prepared, at last, to go home. 'A good day's work?'

'I suppose so, sir,' Marcus answered. 'But I can't help feeling just a little uncomfortable. I mean, we released a murderer, and executed what looked like an innocent man.'

'Yes, that's true,' Pilate said. 'But did we win the game? That's the important question. And if you look at it that way, we did extraordinarily well. We kept the peace. We prevented a riot...'

'And the dead man, sir?'

'Ah, yes,' mused Pilate. 'The dead man. Well, I don't think we'll be hearing from him again. Do you?'

The Robber's Tale

• • • • • • • • • • • •

THE STORY OF A THIEF

*S*ome people say that your whole life flashes before your
eyes just before you die. I don't know if that's true or not,
because I've never faced that situation! But what if it were
true? And what if you had the chance to write it down, or tell
it to someone? Then it might sound something like the story
you are about to read.

It wasn't my fault. Not really. My brother was older than me.
And, you know how it is. You look up to your brother,
especially when you're little. And you want to do what he
does...

Well, my brother was a thief. And even though he was
only eleven or twelve when he started, he got good fast.
He had this innocent face, for a start – round chubby
cheeks that old ladies just loved to pinch. So they trusted
him.

He was quick, too. He could snatch a coin off a table so fast that it looked like his hand had never moved at all!

And best of all, he could talk. Boy, could he talk! One story after another – lie after lie after lie. And all the time with that smile on his face. My brother could talk his way out of anything!

Once – and I had nothing to do with this, I swear! – he stole this chicken from old Simeon's wife. And not just any chicken, of course. But her favourite chicken. The one with the big brown spot on its back! So, there he was, running down the street, with this chicken tucked under his arm, when who should come bustling out of a door in front of us but the old lady herself!'

Now, Simeon's wife was the chief cheek pincher in our village. So when she saw my big brother, right there in front of her, she threw wide her huge arms, and like some enormous lobster, began to flex those fat pinching fingers. Escape? Escape was out of the question, for Simeon's wife was also the widest woman in town. We tried to avoid her. We really did. But our speed and her bulk resulted in one huge collision – and my brother and I found ourselves sitting, dazed, on our backsides before her!

'Now where are you boys off to in such a hurry?' she grinned, pinching his cheeks (and then mine, for good measure). But before either of us could say a thing, she spotted her spotty hen.

The big woman's smile turned down into a frown. But before it could fall into a full-fledged scowl, my brother blurted out, 'We were bringing your chicken back to you. That's why we were in such a hurry! We found it in… Anna's yard. That's right! And we thought maybe it had wandered there or – God forbid! – that old Anna had stolen your chicken. Anyway, we watched her, and when she went into

her house, we grabbed it as fast as we could and ran and...
Here – it's all yours again!'

Simeon's wife just looked at my brother, and then, slowly, her frown turned into a puzzled stare.

'But, Anna?' she pondered, 'Why would Anna want to take my chicken?'

'Jealousy!' my brother jumped back in, eager to save his story. 'That has to be it. After all, it's not everyone who has a chicken that looks like that!'

'That's true,' the old woman nodded. And then she leaned nearer and whispered, 'And I'm sure you're too young to know this, but they say that Anna has always fancied my Simeon – the most handsome man in the village, if I say so myself!'

So she bought the story. And instead of smacking us round the head or dragging us off to the local judge, she pinched our cheeks one more time and rewarded us each with a shiny silver coin!

My brother grinned and strutted as we made our way back home. But I was still a little worried.

'What if she talks to Anna?' I said.

'Oh, I don't think that's going to happen,' he chuckled, as he pulled a piece of woven cloth out from under his shirt. 'I grabbed this out of the old lady's basket,' he laughed. 'Between all the pinching and hugging. It's her own special pattern, and when it gets dark, I know just what we're going to do with it!'

'But it's the Sabbath!' I said.

'That's right!' he grinned again. 'Everybody will be at home, praying and reading and stuff. Everybody but you and me!'

And so, later that night, we crept out of our house and across the village and into Anna's yard. And while I watched, my brother quietly wrung the neck of every chicken in her yard (did I mention that he could be vicious, as well?), and left that piece of cloth behind as 'evidence'.

There was a lot of commotion in the village, the next morning – questions and rumours and accusations. And I understand that the two women never talked to one another again.

As for my brother, he just got better and better at his chosen profession. Pickpocketing, sheep-stealing, breaking and entering – there wasn't anything he couldn't do. And soon, we'd built up a little gang. (Well, he did actually, because, as I've said, I never did any of the *real* stealing. I was a lookout, mostly. Just along for the ride.)

We started moving from place to place. We hit the villages first because they were the easiest. But as folk started to recognize us, we had to aim for the larger towns, and then the cities. Get lost in the crowds – you know what I mean.

Crowds can be a great cover, actually. That's what my brother always said. All those people, bunched together – jostling, bumping, pushing. And if a hand should slip into a pocket, a pouch, or a purse, who would notice? Markets are good, public executions aren't bad, but nothing beats a good old-fashioned religious festival! Nobody's on their guard, you see. They're all feeling good and holy, and they walk around with the mistaken notion that everyone else is feeling good and holy, too!

There was this time, for example, up in Galilee – near the sea – when all these people were listening to this teacher. His name was Jesus and he was another one of those Messiah wannabes. You know – 'Follow me and I will lead you to God.' That sort of thing. Anyway, we were doing pretty well. The crowd couldn't keep its eyes off him, which meant, of course, that they weren't paying attention to us at all!

He was telling this story, about a guy who gets fed up with his dad, runs off with his inheritance, and gambles it all away – or something like that. When the money's all gone, this guy drags himself back home again. You know what the father's going to do – smack him round the head (like Simeon's wife should have done to us!). But no! The father rewards him – gives him rings and robes and a fancy feast! I have to admit it was the most unlikely story I had ever heard. So I glanced over at my brother, to get his reaction. And he was fuming!

I thought, for a moment, that he was angry with me – for listening to the story instead of, you know, attending to the 'business'. But it was the teacher – that's who had him so worked up.

'Now there's the thief!' he muttered. 'He doesn't work – I can promise you that. But somebody's feeding him and taking care of him. He fills their heads with lies, and they love him for it. Let's get out of here!'

And so, even though there were hundreds of purses left to pinch, we headed out across the hills and into the nearest town.

A couple of years went by – I was about eighteen or nineteen by then – and we started to get a little cocky. Success does that to you, and the problem is that you start to get sloppy, too. Soon you start to believe that you can pull off anything – even stealing from the Romans.

That was our big mistake. If we'd stuck to Jews and Samaritans and the odd caravan trader, we'd still be working today. But someone told my brother about all the treasure hidden away in this centurion's house, down in Jerusalem. So he planned it, he broke in, and he grabbed it.

(And as for his beating the centurion nearly to death, well I can't say, can I? I was outside. The lookout. Remember?) Anyway, what we didn't know was that the old boy was retiring, and that a bunch of soldiers had chosen that very night to surprise him with a party. So the surprise was on us and, surrounded, we surrendered. What else could we do?

My brother tried to talk his way out of it. But the Romans didn't really understand our language. So instead of a pinch on the cheek, all he got was a hard smack in the mouth. Then they dragged us off to jail.

When he came to, my brother just sat there, speechless, not for hours, but for days. I'd never seen him so quiet, but each time I tried to say something – you know, start up a conversation, lighten the mood – he growled at me. And, I got the message.

Finally, he spoke. But it wasn't what I expected him to say.

'Did you ever wish you could start all over again?'

I was a little confused. 'You mean, like planning the robbery better? Or staying away from the Romans?'

'No,' he sighed. 'I mean – life. Starting over again. Getting another chance. Like the story that teacher told, about the boy and his father. You remember?'

'But you thought that was stupid,' I reminded him.

'Yeah, well, I guess I never thought I'd need a second chance. I was always so good at talking my way out of things. But now, now that it's all over, I guess I feel different.'

'What do you mean, all over?' I asked. 'We're getting out of here, right?'

And that's when he gave me the 'look'. The big brother to little brother 'look'. The look that said he thought I was some kind of an idiot.

'You don't get it, do you?' he said. 'They're going to kill us. These are the Romans we're talking about. They're going

to drag us out of here, hang us on a cross, and crucify us!'
'But why?' I asked. 'Why? I mean, I didn't do anything.
I was just the lookout. You can tell them that, can't you?'
But my brother just sighed and shook his head and
turned his face again, silent, to the wall.

He was right, of course. Not two days later, they woke us
up, tied each of us to a cross, and before the sun came up,
there we were, just hanging there, waiting to die.
I screamed for a little while. 'It's not my fault,' I pleaded.
'It's not fair!'
But the soldiers just laughed, and the growing crowd
didn't want to know. So after a while, I shut up. It was hard
to breathe, hanging like that, and harder still to talk. Maybe
that's why my brother never said a word.
Time passed. I don't know how much. And then a whole
parade of people came marching up the hill. There was
wailing and weeping on one side and cheering on the other.
And then they raised a third cross up between us.
I turned my head and looked at the guy. He was a mess!
Cuts and bruises all over his body, and blood pouring down
his face. He must have done something awful, I thought.
And as bad as I felt, I was glad I wasn't in his shoes.
And then I looked closer. And I couldn't believe what
I saw.
It was Jesus! You know, the teacher we saw up in Galilee!
I tried to get my brother's attention. But, no, he
wouldn't even look my way. So I thought, hey, why not try
to win a little respect from him, cheer him up, maybe, right
at the end. Show him that I'm not the idiot brother he
always thought I was.
So I turned to this Jesus and I said, 'Hey! Hey! They say
you're the Messiah, right? God's Special Guy. Well, if you're

such a big shot, why don't you do something about this? Why don't you snap your fingers or say the magic word and get us all out of this mess?'

It was good, I thought. Funny, you know. So I glanced at my brother, just to get his reaction. And I couldn't believe it – he was giving me that 'idiot' look again!

'What is wrong with you?' he sighed. 'We're all going to die here. Aren't you afraid of that? And aren't you even more afraid of God, and what he'll do to us? I mean, we're here because we deserve it. We've been thieves all our lives. But look at this man. Look at him! He's done nothing wrong. Not a thing.'

And then he turned to the teacher. And I don't know – maybe it was just sweat – but I'd swear there were tears in my brother's eyes. And that's when he said it.

'Jesus. Jesus, will you remember me when you come into your kingdom?'

And Jesus nodded. And Jesus forced a little smile. And Jesus said, 'Yes. Today, truly, you will be with me in paradise.'

Yeah, I know what you're thinking. I suppose I should have said something, too. But, hey, what for? It was my brother, my brother who was the bad guy. My brother who was the thief. I was just a lookout. Honest. I never did anything wrong, not really. Like I said at the beginning, it wasn't my fault...

The Coward's Tale

●　●　●　●　●　●　●　●　●　●　●　●

THE STORY OF PETER

Sometimes the worst kind of badness is the badness inside
you, the badness you can't seem to fix. You say something
hurtful to somebody. Or you lose your temper. Or you lie about
something. And a minute after you do it, you feel bad, and you
wish you could take it all back. But you can't, because you're
embarrassed or afraid or worried that something worse might
happen if you try to put it right.

Everybody feels that way, sometimes. Peter did. He was
one of Jesus' followers, one of his closest friends. But time and
time again, he found himself doing and saying things that
disappointed Jesus – things he was sorry for later. This story is
about one of those times. And even though Peter tried, he still
couldn't find a way to fix and forgive himself. He needed
someone to do it for him. And fortunately, that someone was

there, hanging on a cross, rising from the dead, and waiting
for him, on the beach.

The fire was warm. And the end of his beard and the edge
of his sandals were just about dry.

His belly was full. The taste of fish lingered in his mouth,
and a crusty bit of bread clung to his moustache.

He'd just had a big catch. His friends sat round about him.
He should have been happy. But he wasn't.

His best friend of all was there, you see. The one who
had died and come back to life. The one he had abandoned
and denied.

There had been a fire, then, as well. And a cold night.
And a silent moon. And in the place of the comrades who
now chattered around him, there sat strangers and enemies.

Peter remembered it well. Too well. It was a serving girl
who had spoken first. She had been gazing through the
flames for some time, trying to catch his eye and to get
a good look at his face. But Peter had sat still, still as stone –
hunched over, silent, afraid. It was her voice that had set
him shivering.

'This man was with him, too!' she pointed. 'With Jesus,
who they arrested!'

Peter held himself tight, to stop the shaking. He was
afraid. He was afraid! The guards. The arrest. The torches.
The fighting. His friends were scattered, his master in
custody. He was afraid! Who wouldn't be? And surely that is
why he had blurted out, almost without thinking, 'Woman!
I do not know the man!'

It was a lie. Of course it was a lie! But if that busybody
hadn't stuck her nose in…

Before he could fashion his excuse, however, another voice called out from the darkness. 'Yes, you're right. I've seen him with Jesus, too! You're one of his followers, aren't you?'

'No! No!' Peter shouted, wishing that somehow he could disappear, hoping to heaven that he could just wake up from this nightmare. 'No, I am not one of them!'

But the strangers would not be quiet. They would not give up. He was the focus of attention, now. And all eyes – he could feel them – were gazing, peering, inspecting and identifying, each and every one trained on him.

Jesus' career had been so public, the miracles so amazing, the crowds so huge. Thousands and thousands of people had seen Jesus and his friends together, with Peter the biggest and noisiest of the bunch. And so it was inevitable that another voice, a third voice, should come to the same conclusion as the rest.

'Yes!' someone called. 'Definitely! He's from Galilee. He's one of them!'

'No!' shouted Peter, his heart racing and his hands sweating.

'No!' he repeated, frantic and afraid. 'I NEVER EVEN KNEW THE MAN!'

And then the rooster crowed.

Jesus had said this would happen. In the midst of Peter's boasting about how he would fight to the death for his master, Jesus had contradicted him.

'No, Peter,' he had whispered. 'Before this night is through, before the cockerel calls to the coming dawn, you will deny that you ever knew me.'

Peter had wept bitterly that day, mixing his tears with the morning dew. And he could find no excuse – not fear, not panic, not fate – to chase away the guilt he felt at having turned his back on his friend.

A chunk of wet sand, caked to the side of his leg, dried through just enough to fall off. But it left behind a filmy, sandy residue that irritated him until he brushed it away. And Peter couldn't help thinking that it was just the same way with his guilt.

They'd met a few times – he and Jesus – since that night. That night before Jesus had died. But now, Jesus was alive again! And the shock and the joy of those meetings had shaken away great chunks of Peter's guilt and shame. But it wasn't all gone. And because Jesus hadn't mentioned his denial, Peter didn't want to bring it up.

And that's why this man with a full belly and warm feet and one amazing, resurrected friend wasn't very happy. There was something he needed to do. Something he couldn't bring himself to say.

There was another reason, too: fish.

When they'd first met – he and Jesus – Peter was a fisherman. But Jesus had promised to make him something else – a fisher of *men*. More than that, Jesus had called him a rock, and when Peter had found the confidence to stand up and say what all the disciples had been thinking – that Jesus was the Messiah – he had received the master's praise for his insight.

But where was Peter now? Sitting on the sand at the side of Lake Galilee. That's where he was. Back where he had started, doing his old job, fishing for fish. But what else was he fit for? What good was a rock that turned to sand at the first whiff of danger?

And how could he be a fisher of men when he couldn't even admit his friendship with Jesus to just three people? Perhaps being a fisher of fish was all he was good for, after all.

A gull cried. The fire popped. Then it belched out a puff

of smoke. Jesus watched the smoke melt into the air, then he turned to Peter and said, 'Simon, son of John, do you love me more than these?'

Surprised by both the suddenness of the question and by the question itself, Peter had to stop and think. 'Do I love him more than these? These what? These other disciples? Well, of course I do. Didn't I say once that even if all the others left him, I would remain?'

And then Peter hung his head in shame. 'But I didn't, did I?' he remembered again. 'I ran and hid like everybody else. And worse.'

Meanwhile, Jesus was poking holes in the sand, waiting for an answer. Peter knew what he wanted to say. But after what he'd done, would Jesus believe him, or just think him the worst kind of hypocrite? And so, with his eyes fixed on the sand, he said, both as quietly and a firmly as he could, 'Yes, Lord, you know that I love you.'

Jesus set the stick down and looked at Peter's face. 'Then feed my lambs,' he said.

This wasn't the response that Peter expected. He thought that Jesus was finally getting round to the 'denial' business. That he'd tell him off, call him a no-good liar or a coward or a phoney. Peter could understand that. It was the least he deserved.

Or maybe, on the other hand, Peter imagined, Jesus would turn to him and say, 'It's all right. I understand. Don't worry about it any more.'

But he didn't do either of those things. All he said was, 'Feed my lambs.'

And then it dawned on him. Perhaps, when Jesus had said, 'Do you love me more than these?' he hadn't meant 'these disciples' at all. Perhaps he'd meant 'these fish'. Well, not the fish themselves, but the fishing gear – the nets and tackle and rope. Maybe Jesus was saying, 'Do you really intend to go back to being a fisher of fish? Or do you want to carry on working for me?'

Peter was going to ask, but Jesus got there first. 'Simon, son of John,' he repeated, 'do you love me?'

There was that question again! Perhaps Jesus hadn't heard him the first time. The answer had been rather quiet. But Peter was feeling more confident now. So he looked at Jesus this time. Well, glanced at him, really. And he gave him the same answer. 'Yes, Lord, you know that I love you.'

'Then feed my sheep,' replied Jesus.

'That's it!' thought Peter. 'He does want me back! He still wants me to be a fisher of men. And he still believes I can be a rock. And now he wants me to be a shepherd, as well – to take care of his followers! He wants me back. He thinks I can do it. Everything is all right again!'

Peter leaped to his feet, ready to throw his nets on the fire, when Jesus took him by the arm, led him away from the others and asked him, one more time.

'Do you love me?'

'Well, this is silly!' thought Peter. 'We've dealt with that already. Surely, Jesus had heard him the first two times. What was the point of saying it... a third time?'

Peter shut his eyes and sighed. Some rock he was turning out to be. More like rocks-for-brains! Peter saw it all, now. Jesus was giving him his job back, yes. But he was giving him something more: A chance to make up for those other three times. A chance to say what he should have said that night. A chance to speak the truth from his heart. A chance to deal with it, once and for all.

Peter opened his eyes and wiped them dry with the back of his hand. Then he looked right at Jesus, right into his

eyes, and said, 'Lord, you know everything. You know that I love you.'

And in return, Jesus smiled a knowing, everything-will-be-all-right kind of smile, and said for the third time, 'Then feed my sheep.'

They wandered slowly back to the others. The fire was warm. Peter's belly was full. He was surrounded by his friends. And now, for the first time in a long time, Peter was happy. Not only because his best friend was alive again. But also because something had come back to life in him, as well.

More Bible Baddies

Contents

The Tempter's Tale

(part 1)

▶ ▶ ▶ ▶ ▶ ▶ ▶ ▶ ▶ ▶ ▶ ▶ ▶

THE STORY OF ADAM AND EVE

I*t's strange, really. The moment we make a wrong choice – the second we buy into badness – it all seems so clear.*

'It's just this once,' we say to ourselves. 'No one will get hurt. It doesn't really matter.' And on and on the excuses go.

But later, when we look back at what we've done – when we have to deal with the shame or the guilt or the consequences – the choice doesn't seem so clear. And, so often, we wonder how we could ever have made such a foolish decision in the first place.

That's certainly how it goes in the story you are about to read – the story of where badness begins. But you may not feel an overwhelming sense of the presence of evil. No, what you will feel instead, I think, is a lingering sense of sadness and regret. And that is as it should be. Because, in a way, this story is also about where badness leaves us in the end.

He hacked at the ground with his rough stone axe. He hacked at the weeds and at the bushes. He hacked till the sweat poured off his forehead and the calluses rose on his palms. He hacked until he could hear his heart pounding in his ears. But still the slithering thing slipped and squirmed away. So he sank down onto a stump and waited for his breath to return and his heart to stop racing. He wiped the sweat from his brow and stared at his hands. And that's when it all came back – the crushing memory of 'before', the pain of the paradise he'd lost.

It was like a bad bruise. It hurt to touch it, but touching it reminded him that it was there. Sometimes a smell would trigger it. Sometimes it would wake him in the night. Today, it was simply the sight of his hands.

Knuckles gnarled and cracked. Palms rough and swollen. Veins running down the backs like tree limbs.

'Were these the hands,' he wondered, 'that once tended a Garden? The hands that stroked the lion's mane and traced the zebra's stripes and danced across the rhino's wrinkled hide as he gave each one its name? Were these really the hands of Adam?'

Sometimes it seemed impossible. Sometimes it seemed too good to have been true. And sometimes he wondered, how had it happened? How had he let it all slip between those rough and dirty fingers?

As if to answer the question, a voice called from across the rocky field.

Yes, he had blamed her once. Blamed her more than once. But he knew now that the fault was his, as well as hers.

Eve called again, and then walked slowly towards him. It was almost impossible to see her as she had once been. The years, and the children, and the endless toil it took just to survive had erased for ever the woman who had danced happily in the Garden.

He shut his eyes. He shut them tight. He shoved his fists into the sockets and for a second, just a second, there she was again. Flesh of his flesh. Bone of his bone. At the dawn of their life together. He remembered touching her hair. And her lips. And tracing the shape of her face with his fingertips. And he remembered the prayer he had prayed. 'Thank you, Creator,' he had said, 'for this face and for this morning, and for all the mornings to come.'

'Adam!' the voice called again. 'Adam, why are you sitting there? Get back to work! We have a family to feed!'

Adam winced. There was still a trace of that other Eve in her voice. The same voice that had called out so many years ago called out across the Garden, 'Adam, come quickly! There is someone I want you to meet!'

That voice was so sweet. The face so innocent and gentle. She skipped towards him, excited like a foal or a fawn. She took his hand (he could feel those fingers, still). And she led him, laughing, to the Knowledge Tree.

There was no reason to be alarmed. No cause for concern. Those words had no meaning then. All was trust and goodness and love. How could he have known?

How could either of them have guessed that their new acquaintance would teach them the meaning of those words – and many more awful still.

The Serpent was a handsome creature. Confident. Persuasive. Poised. There was venom in his words but, at the time, his arguments seemed reasonable.

'So the Creator forbids you to eat from the Knowledge

Tree?' the Serpent had asked. 'He says that if you do, you will die? Well, what does he have to hide? That's what I want to know. And if he truly loves you, why would he want to keep anything from you? I suspect that he's afraid – afraid that if you eat from the tree, then you will know as much as he does! So why don't you taste the fruit and find out for yourselves?'

Even now, even after all the pain and the toil and the years away from the Garden, there was a part of Adam that still wasn't sure. Perhaps the Serpent was right – perhaps the Creator was just jealous of what he knew and did not want to share it. Was it so wrong to want to know? To know evil as well as good?

Adam looked up. His wife was staring at him, and the answer was there, in the lines on her face and in the sadness that never left her eyes. No amount of knowledge could make up for what those eyes had seen: their forced exile from the Garden, the angel with the fiery sword who was there to make sure they could never return, the desolate land they were condemned to till, the murder of one son by another...

Adam looked away and shook his head. His children had often asked him – what did the fruit taste like? Sweet like an apple? Sour like a lemon? How could he have told them the truth? Told them without seeming a fool? That it smelled of decay. That every bite was rotten. That it tasted like death. Death and regret.

Adam pounded his fists against his temples – as he had pounded them a thousand times before.

What if? What if? What if?

What if they had ignored the Serpent? What if they had obeyed the Creator?

What if they had never tasted the fruit?

Would he still be wrestling the lion and running with the

zebra? Would he still wake up each morning in the soft wet grass and trace his finger across Eve's forever beautiful face?

The thought was simply too much to bear. And so he picked up his axe again and began to hack at the earth. Eve grunted her approval and turned to walk away. But once she was out of sight, he listened again for the hissing one.

The Creator had made a promise – Adam remembered. The handsome one, the confident, persuasive creature, would lose his limbs and crawl upon the ground. And one day – surely he was remembering this right – one day, Eve would bear a child who would crush that serpent's head!

But who was this child? And where was this child? All Adam could do was hope. Hope that the Creator's promise would come true. Hope that someone would someday destroy the Serpent. Hope and keep on hacking. Hacking at the ground. Hacking at the bushes. Hacking at the weeds. Because hacking was easier than yearning for what might have been. Because it was better than longing for the life he lost when he left his beautiful Garden.

The Tempter's Tale

(part 2)

● ● ● ● ● ● ● ● ● ● ● ● ●

THE STORY OF JESUS IN THE WILDERNESS

My son is a fan of martial arts films – all that high-kicking kung-fu fighting stuff! And in every one of those films, right at the end, there is always the Big Confrontation between the good guy and the bad guy. But before that – usually quite early on in the film – there is another battle, a smaller battle, where the good guy and the bad guy discover each other's strengths and weaknesses. That's the battle I've chosen to deal with in this story. Not the Big Confrontation between Jesus and the devil – the one at the end of the story where the devil's triumph on the cross is snatched away three days later. The one where he is left holding nothing but an empty tomb. No, this is

*the earlier battle, the quiet one in the desert, where they looked at
each other face to face and tested each other's strength and will.*

*You may notice similarities to Adam's story. That's because
the Bible sometimes calls Jesus the 'Second Adam', come to fight
the enemy that Adam could not beat.*

He scratched at the ground with his cracked, dry fingers.
He scratched at the dirt and the pebbles and the sand. He
scratched out shapes and circles and lines. He was doodling.
He was thinking. He was praying. He was hungry!

For forty days he had fasted. Forty days without food.
Forty days in the desert. Forty days alone. Forty days to chart
the course his life would take. Forty days to consider what it
meant to be the Saviour of the world!

Fasting clears the head, he had been taught. Fasting
helps you to see things more clearly. Fasting brings you
closer to God. And all these things had proved true. But
fasting also makes you sick with hunger – aching, gnawing,
belly-screaming hunger! And maybe that is why he was
suddenly no longer alone.

His companion was handsome. Confident. Persuasive.
Poised. And his suggestions seemed not only sensible, but
kind.

'If you're hungry, why not eat?

'If you're the Saviour of the world, why not use your
power?

'If there are stones, why not turn them into bread?'

Jesus considered the words – considered them carefully.
And he considered the face of his companion. The smile could
not have been more genuine, the eyes more sincere. But the
words – the words were lies. The words were filled with poison.

'There are more important things than bread,' Jesus

replied. 'That's what the scriptures say. There is God, and all that he wants to give us. So if doing without bread helps me to get closer to him, then I am quite happy to go hungry for a while.'

'The scriptures,' his companion nodded. 'Of course. There is a great deal of truth in them, isn't there? Just the other day, I read this remarkable passage about the angels. Shall I tell you about it?'

Jesus just shrugged. He suspected that it would have been pointless to say no. He had it on good authority that his companion was nothing if not persistent.

He sat down beside Jesus and scratched some lines of his own in the sand.

'Imagine this,' he said, tracing out a perfect sketch of a tall and majestic building. 'The Temple in Jerusalem. Do you see it? And here, at the top of the very tallest tower, someone who wants attention. Someone who needs to gather a crowd. Someone who wants to demonstrate God's power. Someone like you, perhaps.'

He sketched a tiny figure at the top of the tower, and then drew a long line down to the ground below.

'Now suppose this someone was to leap from the Temple top. Do you know what the scriptures say would happen? The scriptures say that if that someone was Someone Special – God's own Son, perhaps – then the angels would come to his rescue before his feet ever touched the ground!'

Jesus nodded and traced out the shape of a heart. 'Yes, they do. But the scriptures also say that God loves us, and that we should trust that love. And that it would be wrong to put ourselves in foolish and dangerous places simply to put that love to the test.'

'But what about your mission?' asked the companion, more confident than ever. 'Surely saving the world is your life's work. And if it's the world you want, then I am the one to give it to you.'

He stood up. He waved wide his arms. And a hot wind swept up a desert's full of drawings. Armies and palaces. Treasures and thrones. All that anyone could ever want sprang up before Jesus and stood glittering and gold against the purple sundown sky. And all the while, his companion's words kept echoing in his ears.

'All of this will I give you if you will bow down and worship me!'

But Jesus did not move. For there were other words, as well. Words that he knew from his childhood and before. And these were the words he whispered as he drew one last shape on the ground.

'I will worship the Lord my God and him alone will I serve.'

Jesus looked up. The vision was gone, and so was the smile on his companion's face.

'I don't understand,' he said. 'I offer you the world and you draw an X through it?'

'Not an X,' said Jesus. 'A cross.' And that is when he noticed the blood on his companion's head.

'You're hurt,' said Jesus.

'It's nothing,' muttered his companion.

But as they stared at each other, both of them remembered one more scripture – a promise, an old promise, about a child and a battle and a crushing blow to a serpent's head.

'I will be back,' said the companion.

'I will be waiting,' said Jesus.

And suddenly he was alone again. Considering the course of his life. Thinking. Praying. Doodling. So he scratched at the ground with his cracked dry finger – scratched a circle beside the cross. The shape of the sun as it set? The whole of the moon as it rose? Or the mouth of an empty tomb?

The Trickster's Tale

• • • • • • • • • • • • •

THE STORY OF JACOB

'*You reap what you sow.*'
'*The bad things you do come back to haunt you.*'

Whatever image you choose – gardening or ghost – the story of Jacob looks, at first, like proving these sayings true.

Jacob deceives both his brother and his father to win an inheritance. And, in turn, he is deceived – first by his uncle and then by his own sons. It looks as if the story has come full circle, and Jacob has got what he deserves. The trickster is tricked. The End.

But that's not actually how it goes. Because somewhere along the line, Jacob runs into God. And even though their relationship turns into a bit of a wrestling match, Jacob discovers that God is far less interested in punishment than he is in mercy and forgiveness. So while Jacob still reaps some of

what he sowed and still has to deal with the odd haunting
dream, he also finds something else. He finds a new strength
and renewed faith in God. And that's what makes his story so
compelling.

Jacob held the coat against his face, and rocked gently back
and forth. His tears mixed with the bloody stain. The ragged
rips in the cloth tore holes in his heart. His son, Joseph, was
dead – bloody and torn like the coat, consumed by some
savage beast.

There was nothing that could comfort him. No words to
wail that would make any difference. There was just a hole
where his son had been – a hole that would never be patched
or mended.

Jacob had other sons, of course. But Joseph was special, the
child of his beloved Rachel. He could hear them talking and
laughing outside the tent. Jacob was no fool. He knew they
hated their brother – hated him because Joseph had known he
was special and had not let them forget it. But that was no
excuse. The dead – even the despised dead – deserve respect.

Jacob tried to sleep. He folded Joseph's torn coat – the
coat he himself had made – and tucked it under his head for
a pillow. Then he shut his eyes and prayed that sleep would
come and take his pain away.

But all sleep brought was dreams. And the dreams were
more painful still.

Soon Jacob was dreaming about brothers. Not the noisy
young men outside, but Jacob himself and his twin brother
Esau. His mind whirled back to life at home as a young man…

They had always been rivals. Esau, with his red locks,
hairy arms and strong back, was their father Isaac's favourite.

And Jacob, smaller and rather fragile, was ever under the watchful eye of their mother Rebekah.

At last the time came for Esau to claim his birthright. He was the elder of the two, just, so tradition dictated that blind old Isaac's blessing should be given to him – along with the right to rule the family and inherit the family fortune!

But Rebekah was canny and clever and shrewd, and she was determined that her favourite, Jacob, would receive that blessing instead.

And so the dream went on, as Rebekah's voice echoed around inside Jacob's head.

'Take your father his favourite meal.

'Lower your voice. You'll sound just like Esau.

'Wrap your arms in these goat skins. Your father's blind, but he's no fool. He'll want proof.

'And when he is convinced that you *are* your older brother, that is when you should ask him for his blessing!'

The dream was so clear, so real. Jacob saw himself in the dream smiling a smug smile, delighted. For the trick had worked! And, once given, the blessing could not be taken back!

And he saw his brother, Esau, beside himself with anger. His face matched the colour of his bright red hair. Esau knew there was nothing he could do about what had happened. But he was ready to kill the brother who had tricked him and stolen his birthright, and Jacob knew it.

Jacob woke with a start. He wiped the sweat from his face and rolled over. His sons were still talking and laughing. And as sleep washed over him and the dreams returned, he wished that they would be quiet. He wished that they would just go away.

'Go away!' his mother was telling him. 'Go away as far

as you can. Go to my brother, Laban.'

Jacob went, and discovered that his mother's deceitfulness was something that ran in the family.

Jacob's uncle, Laban, had two daughters. And Jacob fell in love with the youngest almost at once.

Jacob stirred in his sleep as painful images from the past came into his mind...

'Work for me for seven years,' Uncle Laban was telling him, 'and pretty Rachel will be your wife.'

So Jacob worked. It was long, hard, honest labour. But when the wedding day arrived, he was shocked to find a different daughter by his side.

'Leah's the oldest,' Uncle Laban grinned, neglecting to mention that she was by far the plainest, as well! 'It's only fair that she should marry first. But I suppose if you worked, say, another seven years for me, you could marry Rachel, too.'

Jacob had been tricked! Jacob was livid. And it was only now, seeing himself in his dream, that he was able to recognize the same expression that had been on his brother Esau's face.

Trickery or not, Jacob was determined to win Rachel. And seeing as there were no other ugly daughters hanging about, he thought that he stood a decent chance this time. So, in order to marry the girl he truly loved, Jacob worked for another seven years.

Jacob was tossing and turning now and he shivered as his dreams brought back more memories...

Now Jacob was a grown man with wives and a family and servants and flocks of his own. More than anything, he wanted to go back home. But would Esau still want revenge? Would Jacob's life still be in danger? He did not know the answer to those questions. All he could do was return and hope.

When he had reached the borders of his brother's land, Jacob sent his servants ahead of him.

'Take the sheep and the cattle with you,' he told them. 'And if you should meet Esau, tell him that they are a gift from his brother Jacob – a brother who longs to be reunited with him.'

Next, Jacob sent his family – as an expression of his trust and goodwill. So now he was to spend one night alone, at the side of the River Jabbok – a night that would change his life for ever.

It might have been a dream itself, so strange was the experience. But as he watched it all again, Jacob knew that it had been real...

His attacker came from nowhere – out of the dark and the night. He grabbed Jacob round the waist and threw him to the ground. Jacob tore himself free from his attacker and turned to face him. He expected to see a thief, or a madman, maybe. Or perhaps, even, his brother, Esau. But Jacob's attacker was none of those. He was bigger and stronger than any man that Jacob had ever seen. And there was something about him that had made Jacob wonder if he was even human!

Jacob knew he should run away, but there was something inside him that needed to go on wrestling. He had been wrestling all his life, it seemed. Wrestling with his father and his brother and his uncle, Laban. Wrestling to hold on to what he believed was his. And so he held on to his attacker, as well – they wrestled all through the night!

'Who are you?' Jacob cried. 'What do you want?' But his attacker did not answer him. They grunted and struggled and rolled on the ground. And even when the attacker put Jacob's hip out of joint, Jacob did not let go. Finally, as the sun began to rise, Jacob's opponent spoke.

'Let me go!' he said. 'The day is upon us.'

'No!' Jacob answered, struggling for breath. 'I will not let you go unless you give me something.'

'All right, then,' the opponent agreed. 'You will no longer be called Jacob – I will give you a new name. From now on you shall be known as "Israel" for, as the name suggests, you have struggled with God and persisted to the end!'

'Struggled with God?' Jacob wondered. 'But that must mean...' And so he asked. He had to ask. 'Then what is your name?'

Jacob's opponent smiled and said, 'I think you already know the answer to that question.'

And then he was gone!

Jacob fell to the ground and rubbed his aching hip. 'Could it be?' he wondered. Could it really be that he had seen the face of God, wrestled with the Almighty – and lived? And suddenly, everything made sense – the whole of his long, wrestling life. God had a purpose for him. The struggles were all for a reason. To shape him and make him into the man, then the family, then the nation that God had promised to his father, Isaac, and his grandfather, Abraham.

And so Jacob rose and limped across the river, made peace with his brother Esau and returned to the land of promise. It looked as if everything would turn out all right.

But now... now Jacob's dream had become a nightmare. For Joseph, his special son, was dead. And all the struggling and wrestling had been for nothing.

Meanwhile, outside the tent, two of Jacob's other sons listened to him stirring and groaning.

'He's not taking it well,' one son observed.

'What did you expect?' shrugged the other. 'Joseph was his favourite.'

'Perhaps we should have told him the truth – that Joseph was sold into slavery.'

'What? And admit that we were the ones who did the selling? I don't think so, and besides, it's all quite fitting, if you ask me. The old man got up to his fair share of tricks when he was our age. Now the last laugh is on him.'

It wasn't, of course, for the God who wrestled with Jacob had one more trick up his God-sized sleeve. Joseph was on his way to Egypt. And when he arrived, God would help him rise to the top of the kingdom, where he would one day save his family and be united with them again.

But that's another story. About another dreamer. And another set of dreams!

The Bully's Tale

THE STORY OF GOLIATH

The story of David and Goliath is probably one of the best known in the Old Testament.

It's not hard to understand why. The world is full of bullies.

When I was seven years old, my family moved house and – wouldn't you know it – there was a bully living right across the street! I was short and shy and chubby – perfect bully fodder. And I was beaten up regularly.

In those days, parents had but one response to that kind of situation – 'Stand up for yourself, boy! Fight back!'

So, one day, that's exactly what I did. It was hard and it was scary, but I clenched my fists and waved my arms, and the bully ran away!

I was amazed. I was in shock. In fact I was so confused that the only thing I could think of doing was to knock on the *bully's back door and apologize to his mother (did I mention that I was also excruciatingly polite?).*

I'm not sure what I learned from that experience at the time, but I can tell you what I think now.

The bigger we get, the bigger the bullies get, too. So sometimes, somebody (and maybe even the last person you would expect) has to stand up and do something hard and scary. Somebody like Martin Luther King, who dreamed of a day when all people would be treated equally, regardless of their race. Somebody like William Wilberforce, who spent a lifetime arguing that slavery was wrong. Somebody like Mother Teresa, who argued that all people – poor people and sick people and people who were still waiting to be born – deserved our protection and care. And – who knows – maybe someday, even somebody like you!

He hated little things. And maybe that was because he had never really been little himself.

He'd been a baby once, of course. But he was the biggest baby the people of Gath had ever seen! So it was big robes and big sandals and big toys, right from the start. And, 'Don't push that little boy, dear.' And, 'Careful with that pot, child.' And, 'Don't squeeze the kitty so hard, Goliath – you'll hurt him.'

Little things. Little kitties. Little people. The world was full of them! And it didn't take long for them to notice that he was different – and to bring it, constantly, to his attention.

Some children return teasing with humour. Others with sullen stares. But Goliath chose fear. Even the most harmless comment about his size would result in a furious beating

from the big boy. Yes, he was beaten up a few times, himself
– by some of Gath's older lads. But he soon outgrew them
all, and then no one dared challenge the boy who stood
nearly seven feet tall!

'There's only one thing to do with bullies...' his father
finally said. 'The army! That'll sort him out.'

Given his size and his strength, he might have risen high
in the ranks. But his obvious hatred for the 'little generals'
and their 'little rules' kept him marching with the infantry.
In the end, there was only one thing Goliath was good for –
frightening the enemy. And he was very good at that indeed!

He'd strap on his armour – all 125 gleaming pounds of it.

Then he'd pick up his spear – ten feet long, with a ten-
pound iron point.

And finally he would stand at the front of the Philistine
troops – a shining monster of a man.

'A challenge!' he would roar – and his roar rumbled
across the valley to whichever army was camped on the
other side. 'A challenge is what I offer! Send your best man
to fight me. And if he wins,' and here Goliath always had
a little chuckle, 'we shall be your slaves.'

A few men had taken up his challenge. Little men. With
little swords. Goliath always smiled when he remembered
how he had crushed their little heads and left their little
bodies broken and twisted and torn.

Most men, however, never even tried. His presence alone
made their little hearts beat with fear and sent them
retreating to their little tents.

He expected as much today. The Israelites were not just
a little people, they were the littlest of them all! A few
scattered tribes. A puny, ramshackle army. And if what he
had heard was true, they had just one little god to protect
them. It hardly seemed worth the trouble, but he marched

out anyway into the valley of Elah and issued his customary challenge. He anticipated a short day's work. But he had no idea how short it would turn out to be.

The Israelites heard the challenge, as they had every day for the past forty days. And, to a man, they trembled. But someone else heard the challenge, too. Someone who had never heard it before. And it made him angry.

Maybe it had to do with his feelings about his people. Maybe it had to do with his feelings about his God. Or maybe he was just tired of being little.

David was the youngest of eight brothers, after all. And no matter how much courage he had shown, defending his father's flock of sheep, they all still thought of him as the 'runt'. Hand-me-down sandals and pass-me-down robes – that was his lot. And while his older brothers were able to serve as soldiers, the best he could do was to bring them lunch and carry chunks of goat's cheese to their commanders!

'If only,' David dreamed, 'I could do something big, for a change.'

And then he heard Goliath's challenge.

'So what do you get if you beat the giant?' he asked a soldier close by.

'A king's ransom,' the soldier answered. 'And the king's own daughter.'

'Well,' mused David, 'I'm surprised someone hasn't accepted the challenge already.'

And that's when he felt a hand – a big hand – on his shoulder. The hand belonged to his oldest brother, Eliab.

'What are you doing here?' Eliab growled.

'Bread... umm, cheese...' David muttered.

'Excuses, more like it,' Eliab growled again. 'Get back to the fields, where you belong!'

But David did not go back to the fields. No, he crept

along the front lines, talking to one soldier after another, always about the giant. Finally, word got back to King Saul, who asked to see the boy.

The giant meanwhile was still waiting.

'Their little hearts are in their little throats,' he chuckled, in a nasty sort of way. Then he looked down at his shield-bearer. The little man was not chuckling back. In fact, it was all he could do, in the hot noonday sun, to keep himself and the shield standing upright.

'Pathetic,' Goliath muttered, and then wondered if the Israelites would ever send him a challenger.

'So you want to fight the giant?' grinned King Saul.

David had seen that look before. He got it from his big brothers all the time. It was that 'I'm-not-taking-you-seriously-you're-just-a-little-shepherd-boy' kind of look.

So David stood as tall as he could and answered with the straightest face and the deepest voice he could manage.

'Yes, Your Majesty, I do.'

'And what makes you think you can beat him?' the king continued, more seriously now.

David didn't even have to think.

'I have fought lions,' he said. 'And I have fought bears. All to save my father's sheep. And every time, the Lord God has helped me win. I am sure he will do the same with this giant.'

The king didn't know what to do. The boy had courage. The boy had faith. But if he allowed him to fight the giant, the boy would also soon be dead! Still, he needed a champion – any champion! So he made the boy an offer.

'My armour,' said the king, pointing to the other side of the tent. 'At least take my armour. My shield. My sword. My breastplate. Whatever you like! You will need all the protection you can get.'

David looked at the armour. He even tried a piece or two

of it on. But it was much too big and much too heavy for him.

'I have all the protection I need,' he said to the king, at last. 'The Lord God himself will be my breastplate. He alone will be my shield.' And he bowed and turned and walked out of the tent.

Goliath, meanwhile, was tapping one big foot on the ground and humming an old Philistine folk song.

'In another minute, we're going back to camp,' he said to his shield-bearer, who breathed a relieved sigh and thanked every god he could think of. But before he could finish his prayer, a cheer rang out from the Israelite camp. Someone was walking onto the battlefield.

'At last!' Goliath drooled, like a hungry man who has just been told it's dinnertime.

The figure looked small, at first. Goliath put it down to the distance. But the closer he got, the smaller it seemed, until the giant realized, at last, that his challenger was no more than a boy!

'Is this some kind of joke?' he muttered to his shield-bearer. But neither the shield-bearer nor the boy was laughing.

'Or is it...' and here the giant's words turned into a snarl, 'is it some kind of Israelite insult? Do they mock me? Do they make fun of me? Well, we'll see who has the last laugh!'

And then he roared – roared so the ground shook, and the shield-bearer, as well.

'Do you think I am a dog?' he roared. 'That you come at me with this little stick of a boy? Send me a real challenger. Or surrender!'

'I am the real challenger,' said David, in that deep voice he had used before the king. 'And the God I serve is the real God. He will give me the victory today!'

Goliath had heard enough. He grabbed his shield and raised his spear and charged. Little people and little generals and little soldiers. Little things had plagued him all his life! And now this little boy and his little army and his pathetic little god were going to pay. He'd skewer the lad and crush his little head and show everyone what someone big and strong could do!

But as he rushed towards the boy, David calmly reached into his shepherd's pouch. He placed a small stone into his sling and he swung it round his head. Then he prayed that God would make his throw both strong and true.

The stone and the giant sped towards each other. And at the last moment, Goliath caught a glimpse of it – a tiny speck, a minute fragment, so small it was hardly worth avoiding. But when it struck him between the eyes, he roared and he cried and fell crashing to the ground. And that little thing was the last thing that the giant ever saw!

The Rotten Rulers' Tale

▸ ▸ ▸ ▸ ▸ ▸ ▸ ▸ ▸ ▸ ▸ ▸ ▸ ▸

THE STORY OF AHAB AND JEZEBEL

I've often wondered – do baddies really think they're bad? Did Hitler or Stalin ever say to himself, 'I'm responsible for the deaths of millions of people. I must be a real monster!'

Somehow, I doubt it. I reckon that even the baddest of baddies do what the rest of us so often do – they justify the wrong things they have done and then just get on with their lives.

But what if there were baddies who knew exactly who they were? And even found a certain wicked pleasure in their deeds? That's the idea I've tried to explore in this story – with two of the 'baddest' baddies of them all, Ahab and Jezebel.

King Ahab wanted to be wicked. He wanted it in the worst kind of way! But he lacked the courage. And he lacked the imagination. And worst of all, he lacked the will – the 'killer instinct' that true wickedness demands.

His queen, Jezebel, however, lacked nothing. She was, without question, the most wicked woman he had ever met. And this just made things worse. For, given her expertise at evil, her artistic flair for foul play, he could never hope to impress her with any wickedness of his own.

She sensed this, of course (even the most wicked have their compassionate side), and tried her best to cheer him up.

'Who's the wicked one, then?' she would ask playfully, over breakfast.

And Ahab would blush and lower his eyes and answer coyly, 'You don't mean me, do you, darling?'

'Of course I do!' she would coo. 'Who betrayed his own people? Who put my god, Baal, in place of Yahweh, the God of Israel? Who murdered Yahweh's prophets? And who chased his true believers into hiding? It was you, my dear – that's who. Wicked King Ahab!'

'Well, I couldn't have done it alone,' he would mutter in a humble sort of way. 'I had a wonderfully wicked wife to help me.'

'Nonsense!' Jezebel would reply coyly. 'You're quite wonderfully wicked all on your own!'

Then the conversation would turn to the weather (dry, always dry!), or to the state of the economy (failing crops, starving cattle), and ultimately to that pesky prophet Elijah, who had somehow managed to stop the rains from falling.

'If I ever get hold of him,' Ahab would rant, 'I'll murder him!'

'I'll do more than that!' Jezebel would reply. 'I'll torture him – slowly – and stand there and laugh as he dies!'

'I'll rip off his fingers!' Ahab would return.

'I'll tear out his hair!' Jezebel would shriek.

And on and on it would go, until the two of them would collapse in fits of evil laughter. It was, on the whole, a strange sort of relationship. But it seemed to work for them.

One morning, however, King Ahab failed to appear at the breakfast table. And when Jezebel found him – on his bed, in his room – he had a woefully unwicked expression on his face.

'What's the matter, dear?' Jezebel chirped. 'Run out of prophets to kill?'

'No,' Ahab sighed. 'Something much worse than that. It's the vineyard, next door.'

'Naboth's vineyard?' queried Jezebel. 'What could possibly be the problem with Naboth's vineyard?'

'It's in the way!' Ahab moaned. 'That's the problem! My little garden is much too small. I want to put in some cabbages, next year. And some sprouts. And two more rows of those little potatoes you like so well. But his stupid vineyard is right smack up against our wall. I've offered to buy it. I'd give him more than what it's worth. But the selfish so-and-so refuses to sell! So what can I do?'

Jezebel tried hard to hide her frustration. There were plenty of things that Ahab could do. He was king, after all! And a wicked king (or a wicked wannabe!), as well.

The answer was obvious. But would telling him, straight out, snuff out the spark of true villainy she had worked so hard to ignite? Would it fracture his already brittle evil self-esteem? In the end, she decided to take matters into her own hands.

'Leave it to me,' she said quietly. Then she turned the conversation to the weather.

Later that day, while Ahab was out digging in the garden,

Jezebel sneaked into his chambers and picked up his pen. She wrote letters to all the elders and noblemen in Naboth's home town. She forged Ahab's signature (she'd had plenty of practice – so it was perfect!). And she marked each letter with Ahab's special seal.

My dear friend and servant,
     I have a favour to ask of you. Would you proclaim a day of fasting – a special, holy day – in your town? Would you be so kind as to invite my neighbour, Naboth, to this event? (He has a lovely vineyard, don't you think?) Please give him the most prominent seat at the event – a place where everyone can see him? And then would you hire two villains (I have names and references) to stand up in the middle of the ceremony and accuse Naboth of some heinous crime? Blasphemy against his god, perhaps. And disloyalty to the king. And then, and I hope this is not asking too much, would you drag Naboth from that place and stone him to death?
     Thank you very much for your consideration. I do hope that this will not be too much of an inconvenience. As always, my concern is for your continued health and well-being, which will be assured by your prompt response to this request.
     Regards,
     Ahab, king of Israel

Jezebel cackled and clapped her hands. There was a joy to pure evil that never failed to delight her. Naboth would die (she had never liked the look of his vineyard anyway!). Ahab would get his plot of land. And the local noblemen would be convinced, once and for all, of her husband's utter and total wickedness. She couldn't wait to see the look on his face.

Her wait lasted only a few days. Ahab appeared at breakfast, one morning – a changed man.

'I'll have two eggs for breakfast, this morning,' he grinned. 'And – why not, by Baal! – a few rashers of bacon, as well!'

'So what's got into you?' asked Jezebel innocently.

'Haven't you heard, my dear?' Ahab beamed. 'Naboth is dead. His widow wants to sell. And now, at last, his vineyard will be mine!'

'How wonderful!' said the queen. 'So tell me – how did poor Naboth die?'

'It was most unusual.' Ahab mumbled through a mouthful of egg. 'Blasphemy. Treason. Not very neighbourly, if you ask me. But then the rumour is that the charges were trumped-up. As if...' and here the king's chewing became more deliberate, 'as if someone truly wicked had it in for him.' And here he stared at his queen.

Jezebel could contain herself no longer. She blushed and she nodded, like a schoolgirl caught with a love note.

'Yes, my darling, I was the one who arranged it. I thought, at first, that it might be better to leave it to you – wicked man that you are. But you were so miserable! And in the end, I just wanted to see you happy again.'

Ahab held up his hand. 'Enough,' he said, solemnly. There were tears in his eyes, and little yellow bits of egg on his trembling lips. 'I have been blessed with the most exquisitely evil wife in the whole world. What more could a wicked king ask for?'

And then he gave Jezebel a big, sloppy, eggy kiss. It was, on the whole, a disgusting thing. But it seemed to work for them.

Ahab's celebration was short-lived, however. For, as he strolled through his new vineyard later that day, he was surprised by an unexpected guest.

'Elijah!' Ahab cried. 'What are you doing here?'

The king's voice was shaking. Shaking with anger, as he remembered the threats he had made against this man. And shaking with fear, as well – for this was the man who had stopped the rain.

'I have a message for you from my God,' Elijah solemnly replied. 'The God who sent a drought upon this land. The God who was once your God, too.

'The Lord says, "You have murdered poor Naboth, and now you want to steal his property, as well! I promise you this: on the very spot where the dogs lapped up the blood of Naboth, they shall lap up your blood, too." '

Ahab's shaking was all fear now. 'Naboth... no... you don't understand.' He tried to explain. 'Jezebel... it was all her doing.'

' "And as for your wife, Jezebel," the prophet continued, "the dogs will do even more. They will chew her to pieces and leave so little behind that even her dearest friends will not be able to recognize her!" '

Ahab wanted to be wicked. He really did. He wanted to turn his evil threats into reality. He wanted to rip off Elijah's fingers and tear out Elijah's hair and torture Elijah and murder him. But it's hard to be wicked – really hard – when what you actually feel like doing is running away!

Ahab was scared – more scared than he had ever been in his whole sorry life. So he ran from the vineyard and hid in his room and wept and wailed and hoped that Jezebel wouldn't notice.

The noise was hard to miss, however, and Jezebel was humiliated by her husband's behaviour – a feeling that turned to disgust when he told her his battle plans over breakfast, one morning.

'It looks as if we'll have to fight the Syrians,' he said thoughtfully, as he lifted a dripping spoonful of porridge to his mouth. 'And the prophets have told me that I will die in the battle.'

'Not Elijah, again!' Jezebel groaned. 'If I hear the story about the dogs one more time…'

'No, no! Not just Elijah,' Ahab interrupted. 'But the prophet Micaiah, as well.' And Ahab dropped the spoon back into the bowl. 'But here's the thing,' he went on. 'I think I have outsmarted them with a plan so devious that I am sure you will approve. When I go into battle, tomorrow, I will not be dressed as Ahab, king of Israel. I will wear a disguise! The Syrians will try to kill some other poor fool and I shall escape, unharmed!'

Jezebel was appalled. And so upset that she could not eat a single mouthful more. After all her work, all her training, all her coaxing and encouraging and example-setting, had it come down to this? Her husband was not evil. Her husband was not wicked. He was a nasty little man, at best. And a coward, as well!

'All right, my dear,' she said, very quietly. 'Whatever you think is best.' But inwardly she hoped that she would never have to look at that face again.

Her wish came true, of course. Ahab disguised himself, just as he said he would. But a stray arrow struck him, anyway. He bled to death in his chariot, and when his servants washed the chariot down, they did so on the same spot where Naboth had died. And so Elijah's prophecy came true.

Some years later, a civil war broke out in Israel. The king's heirs and the king's commanders fought for control of the country, and in the end it was a man named Jehu who was victorious. Early one morning, he rode to Jezebel's house.

She knew he was coming. It was inevitable. So she put on her best clothes and make-up. 'He's a ruthless man,' she thought. 'Perhaps I can win him over and make him more ruthless still.'

But Jehu was ruthless enough already. When he saw Jezebel at the window, he called out to her servants and demanded that any who were loyal to him should seize her and throw her to the ground.

There were plenty of volunteers, as it happened, and while Jehu went into the house and had something to eat, the dogs breakfasted on the body of the dead queen.

'Someone had better bury that woman,' Jehu said to one of his servants, when he had finished. But when the servant went out into the street, there was nothing left to do. Elijah's prophecy had come true again – all that was left of Jezebel was her skull and her feet and the palms of her hands!

The Wicked Granny's Tale

THE STORY OF ATHALIAH

My grandmother was pretty typical, as far as grannies go. She filled me up with sweets and cake and sugared cereal. She bought me far too many Christmas presents. And when I slept overnight at her house, she let me stay up well past my bedtime to watch scary movies!

She was also, for a very short time, one of my Sunday school teachers. And all I can imagine is that her passion for those Saturday night 'Mummy and Monster' movies must have spilled over onto her Sunday mornings, because she loved telling the most bloodthirsty Bible stories! Yes, that's when I first heard about Eglon and his sword-sucking stomach. Samson and his crushing strength. And Judas, with his bowels gushing all over the ground. (I didn't even know what a bowel was, at the time – I just loved the way my grandmother said it!)

Then, of course, there were the inevitable stories about Ahab, the evil Israelite king, and his foreign wife, Jezebel, who taught God's people all about the strange idols of her homeland, and persecuted the prophet Elijah, and whose blood was lapped up by the dogs when she died. And finally, there was Athaliah, the daughter of this wicked couple, who murdered her own grandchildren to gain control of the throne.

A wicked granny? An evil grandma? It seemed a strange thing, especially coming from my own grandmother's lips. Did it have any effect on me? Well, let's just say that, from that time on, I looked a little more suspiciously at the Frosted Flakes she fed me. And when those scary movies were over, I insisted on sleeping with the lights on – and my back right against the wall!

Sweet and gentle. Wise and kind. Kitchens rich with the smell of fresh-baked treats. That's what grannies are like!

But Athaliah was not your typical granny.

She was cruel and ambitious, deceitful and sly. And she had never baked a biscuit in her life! Evil plots were her speciality, and she cooked one up the moment she heard that her son, the king, was dead.

She gathered her guards around her. She whispered the recipe in their ears. And even though they were used to violence and to war, they could not hide the horror in their eyes.

'Yes, I know they're my grandsons,' Athaliah sneered.

'But I want you to kill them, so that I am sure to inherit the throne!'

Athaliah was not your typical granny. And she hadn't been much of a mother either. So perhaps that is why her daughter, Jehosheba, was not surprised when she peeped into the hallway and saw soldiers marching, swords drawn, towards the nursery door.

Jehosheba had a choice. She could rush to the nursery and throw herself in front of her little nephews – and be killed along with them, more likely than not. Or she could creep back into the room from which she'd come, and try to save the king's youngest son, Joash – the baby she'd been playing with when she had heard the soldiers pass.

The screams from the nursery answered her question. She was already too late, and she cursed the palace guards for their speed and efficiency. Speed was what she needed, as well, for she could hear the guards' voices coming her way.

'Did we get them all?'

'We'd better get them all!'

'The queen will have our heads if we've missed one.'

And so they burst into each room, one by one, down the long palace hall, and Jehosheba just had time to wrap her hand round the baby's mouth and duck into a cupboard.

'Don't cry,' she prayed, as the soldiers grunted and shuffled around the room. 'Please don't cry.'

'No one here,' someone said, at last. But Jehosheba stayed in that cupboard, as still as a statue, long after they had left the room. Then she wrapped up the baby in an old blanket and bundled him off to her home near the Temple.

Athaliah stared sternly at her soldiers.

'So you killed them? Every last one?' she asked.

'Every last one,' they grunted back. Athaliah's stare turned into an evil grin.

'Then tell me about it,' she ordered, 'and don't leave out one tiny detail.'

When the guards had finished their story, Athaliah sent them out of the room. Then she tossed back her head and cackled.

'At last. At last! AT LAST! Queen of Judah. Mother of the nation. That has a nice ring to it. And my parents... my parents would be so proud!'

Jehosheba's husband, Jehoiada, however, had a very different reaction.

'Well, what did you expect?' he fumed, when Jehosheba told him about the murder of their nephews. 'With a father like Ahab and a mother like Jezebel...'

'But I'm HER daughter!' Jehosheba protested. 'You don't mean to say...'

'No. NO!' Jehoiada assured her, as he wrapped his arms around his wife. 'I didn't mean that at all. You are a wonderful mother – a good woman who trusts in the God of Israel. And because of your love and courage, little Joash here is still alive.'

'The true ruler of Judah,' Jehosheba added. 'If only the people knew. You're the high priest. Perhaps you could tell them...'

'Even if they knew, they would do nothing.' Jehoiada sighed. 'Athaliah is much too powerful, and they are still entranced by the false gods she worships. No, we must wait – until they have seen through her evil ways. Then, and only then, dare we show this little fellow to them. Meanwhile, we shall hide him here, in the high priest's quarters, in the Temple of our God. For this is the last place your wicked mother will want to visit.'

One year passed. And while little Joash learned to crawl and then to walk, his evil grandmother was busy murdering anyone who dared to take a step against her.

Two years passed. And as Joash spoke his first words and toddled around the Temple, Athaliah sang the praises of the false god Baal and offered him the blood of human sacrifice.

Three years, four years, five years passed. And as Joash grew into a little boy, the people of Judah grew tired of Athaliah's evil ways.

Six years passed. And when Joash was finally old enough to understand who he was, Jehoiada decided that the time had come to tell the nation, as well.

'We must be very careful,' he explained to his wife. 'The palace guards are finally on our side, but your mother still has some support among the people. We mustn't show our hand too soon.'

'So how will you do it?' Jehosheba asked.

'On the sabbath, it is the usual custom for two thirds of the palace guard to stay at the Temple while the others return to the palace to protect the queen. Tomorrow, however, the bodyguards will leave as expected, but they will not go to the palace. Instead they will return to the Temple by another route and help to protect young Joash, should anything happen.'

'Ah!' Jehosheba smiled. 'So Joash will be surrounded by the entire palace guard – while my mother will be left with no soldiers to carry out her orders!'

'Exactly!' Jehoiada grinned back.

When the sabbath came, the people gathered in the Temple, as usual, to worship the God of Israel. But there was nothing usual about what happened at the end of the service. Jehoiada, the high priest, led a little boy out in front of the crowd. Then he placed a crown on that little boy's head. And while the palace guard gathered round the child, the high priest shouted, 'Behold, people of Judah! Behold your true king – Joash, son of Ahaziah!'

All was silent for a moment, and then someone cheered. Someone else joined in and soon the cheering filled the Temple and echoed from there to the palace, where Athaliah was waiting, and wondering what had happened to her guards.

She was old and frail, now, but as wicked and as stubborn as ever!

'What's going on? What's all the noise about?' she muttered, as she hobbled out of the palace and across to the Temple.

'Out of my way! Get out of my way!' she ordered. And the crowd parted before her. And that's when something caught her eye – a glint, a gleaming from the little king's crown.

'What's the meaning of this?' she glared. 'This looks like treason to me!'

'Not treason, Athaliah,' said the high priest, 'but the true king of Judah restored to his rightful throne – Joash, your grandson!'

'My grandson?' Athaliah shuddered. 'But I thought... I mean... my soldiers... they told me...'

'That they had murdered them all?' asked Jehoiada. 'Is that what you meant to say? Well, in their haste to fulfil your wicked ambition, they missed one – the one who stands before you now, the true king of Judah!'

'Treason!' shouted the old woman again, but her words were stifled by the palace guards who quickly surrounded her.

'Where are we going? What are you doing?' she demanded to know, as they led her away. 'I'm an old woman – a grandmother – don't push me!'

'Don't worry, granny,' one of the guards whispered in her ear. 'This won't take long. Remember what you had us do to your grandsons all those years ago? Well we're going to do the same thing to you now!'

Athaliah shrieked, but only the guards heard her final cry, for the crowds were still cheering – cheering for Athaliah's grandson and for the end of her wicked reign.

The Proud Man's Tale

▶ ▶ ▶ ▶ ▶ ▶ ▶ ▶ ▶ ▶ ▶ ▶

THE STORY OF HAMAN

*P*ride's a funny thing. At first, it doesn't seem all that bad. Self-esteem with 'attitude' – that's what it looks like. But there's a difference.

Self-esteem is all about appreciating yourself for who you really are. It's based on honesty and truth. Pride, however, is rooted in self-deception, in a lie. It's all about convincing yourself that you're smarter or stronger or more important than you really are.

Take Haman, for example. He thought he was so important that he could destroy an entire race of people just because one member of that race had offended him. And, to be fair, he almost got away with it.

Ironically, though, it was that very same pride which tripped Haman up in the end. His confidence in his own *cleverness and power blinded him to the possibility that someone might actually be able to wreck his plans.*

And maybe that's the way it is with every kind of badness. At first, it looks as if the victims are the only ones who get hurt. But, in the end, the people who carry out the evil deeds are sometimes affected just as badly.

Haman walked through the King's Gate, nodding and waving as he went. The faces were familiar – royal officials, noblemen, important people, all of them, with whom he had worked and plotted and argued and fought. There were friends and there were enemies. There were wise men and there were fools. There were those who looked upon him with admiration and those who could barely hide their disgust. But each of them bowed as he passed, for Haman was now the second most powerful person in all of Persia – King Xerxes' right-hand man.

Haman grinned. And Haman strutted. A peacock would have struggled to match his pride. And then Haman came to the man at the end of the line.

'Ah yes, Mordecai,' he reminded himself. 'Mordecai the Jew. The one who uncovered a plot to kill the king – or something like that.' And he glanced at the man and tilted his head, ever so slightly, as if to say, 'Now. Now is the time for you to bow.'

But no bow came. Nor even the slightest hint of honour.

'I'm sorry,' said Mordecai. 'I bow to no man, but to the Lord God alone.'

Haman did nothing. He did not frown. He did not scowl. He did not stop and shout and swear. No, his face showed no emotion whatsoever. He simply walked on, careful to maintain his dignity. But inside, Haman was furious!

'How dare he?' Haman fumed. 'I will not stand for this insult! Mordecai, and all his people, will pay for the way he treated me today!'

And that is why, in the very first month of the next year, Haman went to see the king.

'Your Majesty,' he said, 'there is a certain group of people in our land – people who are different from the rest of us. They worship a different god. They keep different customs. And sometimes those customs require them to break our laws. They are the Jews, Your Majesty, and it seems to me that it would be in your best interest to have them – shall we say – 'removed' from your kingdom. I feel so strongly about this, in fact, that I would be willing to put up ten thousand talents of my own silver to pay for their destruction.'

King Xerxes considered Haman's request. Then he took off his signet ring and gave it to his right-hand man.

'Do as you wish,' he said. 'And you can keep your money. If these people are as dangerous as you say, then it is the king's business to deal with them. Set the date. Seal the orders with my ring. And let the Jews be destroyed.'

Haman did as the king commanded. He wrote out orders for the destruction of the Jews and, being a superstitious man, he cast lots to determine on which day it should happen. When the lot fell on the twelfth month – the month of Adar – Haman was just a little disappointed. He would have to wait nearly a year for his revenge. And then he smiled, for the long wait meant that he would have the chance to gloat every time he walked past the King's Gate – every time he saw his insolent enemy, Mordecai.

What Haman did not know was that the God of Mordecai and his people had plans, as well. For, in spite of all his pride and self-importance, there was a tiny piece of information that the king's right-hand man did not possess.

And how could he, for it was unknown to the king, as well. But Mordecai knew it. And so did Mordecai's God. For it had to do with Mordecai's cousin, Hadassah, the most beautiful girl in the land!

Hadassah's mother and father were dead. So Mordecai had raised her, treating her like one of his own daughters. When King Xerxes had decided he needed a new wife, beautiful girls from all over the country came to Xerxes' harem. Among them was Hadassah, sent by Mordecai. He had given her a Persian name – Esther. And he had told her that she must, by no means, reveal that she was a Jew. (This was Mordecai's big secret.) And when the time had come for the king to choose his bride, Esther's beauty so overwhelmed him that the crown was placed on her head – and a Jewish girl became queen of all Persia!

When Mordecai heard about Haman's plot, he went immediately to Esther's palace. He stood outside the gates. He tore his clothes. He wept and he wailed. At once, Queen Esther sent her servant Hathach to find out what was the matter. Mordecai sent her this message: 'Haman plans to kill all the Jews in Persia. You must go to the king and stop him!'

Esther sent a message back. It was not encouraging. 'You don't understand,' it read. 'I cannot go to the king unless he summons me. To go uninvited would be certain death! And I have not heard from him for a month.'

Mordecai's response was brief and plain: 'Don't think for a minute that you will escape just because you are the queen. If you do nothing, you will perish with the rest of us. But is it not possible that the Lord God has put you in your position for just such a time as this?'

So Esther agreed to go to see the king. She went uninvited and unannounced. And even though he could have put her to death for doing so, he was so taken with her beauty that he extended his golden sceptre in her direction and invited her to enter his throne room.

'What do you want, my dear?' King Xerxes asked.

'Only that you and your right-hand man, Haman, should join me for dinner,' she replied.

And so it was arranged. When he received the invitation, Haman was more puffed-up than ever.

'Look!' he said to his wife, Zeresh. 'Look!' he said to all his friends. 'An invitation to Queen Esther's table. Why, it's almost like I'm one of the family!'

So Haman went to dinner, and, as they were sipping their wine, King Xerxes turned to his queen and said, 'So tell me, my dear, why have you invited us here? I'll wager that there's something you want. You only have to ask, you know, and half my kingdom would be yours!'

Esther blushed and then she answered, mysteriously, 'My request is simple. Come again, tomorrow – you and your right-hand man, Haman – and I will tell you what I want.'

The king was intrigued. He liked this little game. And so, once again, he agreed.

Haman, meanwhile, couldn't believe his luck! Dinner at the queen's table two days in a row! But when he left the palace and passed the King's Gate, his mood turned suddenly sour. For there was Mordecai, again – Mordecai who refused to bow before him.

'You just wait!' Haman muttered to himself. 'The time will come when you will fall before me, begging for your life!'

He was still muttering when he arrived home. So his wife suggested a simple solution.

'Why wait till the end of the year to have Mordecai executed?' she asked. 'If he troubles you so, why not go to the king, first thing in the morning, and ask him to hang

Mordecai? Then you can enjoy your dinner with the queen and not worry about having to look on that insolent man's face again.'

Haman smiled – just a little at first. Then a huge grin broke out all over his face.

'Yes! Excellent!' he cried. And just so that everything would be ready, he ordered his servants to build a gallows, seventy-five feet high, in his own back garden!

The next morning, Haman strutted off to the king's palace, whistling as he went. There was no reason for Xerxes to deny his request. He was the king's right-hand man. So the order would be given, Mordecai would be executed, and this would be the happiest day of Haman's life!

But, once again, there was something that Haman did not know. Something he could never have guessed. Something that the God of Mordecai and his people would use to ensure that Haman's day did not turn out so well, after all.

King Xerxes had suffered through a sleepless night. And every time King Xerxes could not sleep, he ordered one of his servants to read to him from the *History of Persia*. And it just so happened that the passage the king's servant read on that night – the night before Haman's morning visit – was the passage that described how Mordecai had uncovered a plot to kill the king!

'Tell me,' King Xerxes said to his servant. 'Was Mordecai ever rewarded for this noble deed?'

'Not that I can remember,' answered the servant.

So the next morning, when Haman presented himself before the king, Xerxes asked him a question.

'What would you do if you wanted to honour a nobleman who had served you well?'

Puffed up as he was, Haman naturally assumed that the

king was referring to him. So he smiled broadly and offered the following suggestion: 'Take a royal robe that you yourself have worn and a royal horse that you yourself have ridden. Put the robe on the man, put the man on the horse, and then have some other royal official parade him through the city, shouting, "This is what happens to a man who earns the king's pleasure!" '

'An excellent idea!' the king shouted. 'Now I want you to do all that for Mordecai!'

'Mordecai?' Haman choked.

'Yes, Mordecai!' the king repeated. 'Put my robe on his back. Put him on my horse. And walk before him, announcing to everyone what happens to the man who earns my pleasure!'

Haman nodded. Haman bowed. Haman tried very hard not to cringe. Then Haman did what the king commanded, growing angrier with every royal hoofbeat!

When he returned home and told his wife what had happened, she sighed and shook her head.

'It would be foolish to ask for his execution, now. The God Mordecai serves must be very powerful, indeed. The best you can do is enjoy your dinner with the queen and pray that nothing worse happens.'

So Haman went to Queen Esther's palace. But he did not strut. And he did not whistle. He walked with his head lowered, hoping to avoid the wrath of Mordecai's God.

All seemed well at dinner, however. There was laughing and there was joking and Haman's mood began to brighten. Then, over a goblet of wine, King Xerxes turned to his wife and asked, 'So why have you invited us again, my dear? Tell me what you wish for. You may ask for anything – up to half of my kingdom – and it will be yours.'

Queen Esther's suddenly looked serious. Tears filled her eyes.

'Your Majesty,' she said, 'there is someone who wants to destroy me – me and all my people. He has already signed the orders, the date has already been set, and unless you do something to spare us, in the twelfth month, the month of Adar, we will all die!'

The king's face turned serious, too – then red with rage.

'Who has done this thing?' he shouted. 'Tell me and he is the one who will die!'

Esther turned her head slowly and looked straight at a trembling Haman.

'I know this may come as a surprise,' she said, 'but I am a Jew, Your Majesty. And the person who wants to kill me – me and all my people – is your own right-hand man.' And then she pointed. 'It is Haman.'

King Xerxes banged his fist on the table, spilling his wine. He loved his wife – his beautiful wife. And yet, he had signed the order. So he stormed out into the garden to think.

Haman was no fool. He could see what was coming. So when Queen Esther rose from the table and walked away to wait on her couch, he followed her, then threw himself on the couch beside her, begging for mercy. It was at that moment that the king returned to the room.

'What is this?' he cried. 'First you want to kill my wife, and now you make advances to her?'

'No, Your Majesty...' Haman stuttered. But before he could finish his sentence, King Xerxes had called for his guards.

'Reverse the order to destroy the Jews,' he announced. 'And put this man to death, instead!'

'As you wish, Your Majesty,' said the chief guard. And then he added, 'There is already a gallows prepared. At Haman's house, in fact. Rumour has it that he built it for Mordecai, who saved the king's life.'

'Then hang Haman on it!' the king commanded. 'And let this be a lesson for anyone who displeases the king!'

So Haman was hanged, the Jews were saved, and Queen Esther became a hero to her people – a hero whose deeds are celebrated to this day!

The Traitor's Tale

• • • • • • • • • • • •

THE STORY OF JUDAS

So why did he do it? Why did Judas betray Jesus? People have been asking that question ever since those thirty pieces of silver changed hands. And they have come up with a lot of different answers.

Some have suggested that even though Judas was a follower of Jesus – one of his twelve disciples – he simply misunderstood what Jesus was all about. Others have pointed to the money. Or to the influence of the devil. And some have argued that the reason was political – that Judas was originally part of a revolutionary movement that wanted to overthrow the Romans and believed that Jesus would help that cause. And that the betrayal was a result of Judas' frustration when he realized that was not Jesus' intent at all. Finally, there are those who suggest that it was all somehow God's fault – that someone had *to do the deed and it was Judas' fate to be the one.*

As you will see in the following story, I think there is a case to be made for some of these arguments. Except for the last one, that is.

Judas made a decision. He may have been tempted to do it. But he was not forced. Not by God. Not by fate. Not by anyone. His motives may have been pure, they may have been selfish, they may have been confused. But the inescapable fact is this: regardless of Judas' reason for betraying Jesus, that betrayal resulted in Jesus' death.

'He's just not practical!' moaned Judas. 'I think my objection basically boils down to that.'

Judas' companion nodded his head, sympathetically. 'I can see your problem,' he said. 'The man is unfamiliar with the ways of the world.'

'Exactly!' Judas agreed, banging his hand on the table. 'I knew you would understand.' The disciple liked this man. He was a minor official on the Temple staff – the assistant to the assistant to the assistant of the high priest, or something like that. Judas had met him quite by chance, but they had 'clicked' almost at once. The man was confident, persuasive, poised. And best of all, he seemed to sympathize with the disciple's ever-growing frustration.

'Lofty sentiments. High ideals,' the companion went on. 'But it takes more than that to change the world, doesn't it?'

'It's what I've been saying for years,' the disciple sighed. 'But no one wants to listen. Least of all him! We need a power-base, I argue. We need to solidify our following. We need a realistic plan...'

'You need money,' added the companion.

'Money!' the disciple sighed again. 'Don't talk to me about money. Talk to him! He treats it like it was leprosy! No, I take that back – he treats lepers better than he treats your average rich man.'

The companion leaned forward, intrigued. 'How so?'

Judas sighed. 'Where do I start? There are so many examples. All right, here's one:

'This fellow comes along, one day. He's rich – it's obvious. His clothes. His jewellery. The way he walks and holds his head. He wants to join us, so he asks Jesus what he has to do. No, no, first he calls Jesus "Good Teacher". That's it. And Jesus has to go on and on about nobody being good but God. I mean, give me a break. Jesus is about as good as they come. But can he take a compliment? Can he just get on with the conversation? No.'

'The point, my friend?' the companion interrupted. 'What is the point?'

'Yes, well, after all the "song and dance" about goodness, this fellow asks Jesus what he needs to do to get into the kingdom of heaven. Jesus tells him all the obvious stuff: obey the commandments, love your neighbour, blah, blah, blah. The man says he's done all that (the rest of us look at each other and roll our eyes—"Yeah, right!"). But instead of challenging him on that, Jesus tells him that there is just one more thing he needs to do. He has to sell everything he has, and give it the poor.'

'And…?' the companion asked, leaning even further forward.

'What do you think?' the disciple shrugged. 'He walked away.'

'And did Jesus go after him?'

'Of course not!' sighed Judas. 'He just turned to the rest of us and went on about how hard it is for rich men to get into

the kingdom of heaven. "Harder than squeezing a camel through the eye of a needle." Those were his exact words.'

The companion stroked his chin. 'That concerns me,' he said seriously. 'It doesn't seem right, somehow.'

Now the disciple leaned forward. 'You know, there were a few of us who thought the same thing. I don't know about you, but I have always been taught that wealth is a sign of God's blessing. Not Jesus! He acts as if it's some kind of curse.'

'Unless one uses it to help the poor,' the companion added.

'Well, yes... and no,' Judas sighed. 'There was this other time. A woman came to Jesus and started to pour this bottle of incredibly expensive perfume on his feet.'

'Quite a luxury!' the companion observed.

'Exactly,' agreed Judas. 'And the first thing that came to my mind was our little treasury. We needed funds desperately, and I, of all people, knew that.'

'What with you being the treasurer?' the companion interrupted.

'Just so. Anyway, I knew that I would get nowhere if I suggested selling the perfume and putting the profits in our money bag. So I simply suggested that we sell it and give the money (well, some of the money!) to the poor. Foolproof, I thought – a perfectly reasonable plan. But, no! Jesus has a different idea. "The poor will always be with us," he says. "But I am only going to be here for a short while." Who knows what he meant by that? "So leave the woman alone and let her get on with it."

'Now you tell me. Is there any consistency in that, whatsoever? Anything sensible? Anything practical? On the one hand, he accepts this expensive gift. On the other, he condemns rich men for their wealth.'

The companion shook his head. 'It makes no sense to me – particularly since there are rich men who belong to your little band of followers. What about Levi, the one they call Matthew?'

Judas rolled his eyes. 'The tax collector. Yes, well, we seem to specialize in those. Matthew. Zacchaeus. But it's always the same drill: make friends with Jesus. Give all your money away. Pay back the ones you've cheated. Help the poor. And by the time it's over, there's nothing left for our little treasury. And I should know…'

'What with you being the treasurer,' the companion said again.

'Exactly!' sighed the disciple. 'And if Jesus ever took the time to look into our money bag, he'd understand what I have to deal with. It takes more than a penny or two to change the world. And besides, I don't trust him.'

'Jesus?' asked the companion.

'No! No! Matthew!' replied Judas. 'I think he's still in league with the Romans. It makes sense, doesn't it? He collected taxes for the Romans for all those years. And now I catch him taking notes on what we're up to. Watching, listening, and then scribbling things down! He's spying for them, I'm sure of it.'

'I can see why you might be concerned,' the companion said. 'The Romans are a worry.'

'The main worry!' Judas cried. 'It's why I joined up with Jesus in the first place. If he is the Messiah – and the miracles alone are enough to convince me of that – then he will eventually destroy the Romans and our land will be free again. I just wish he'd get on with it. Forget all this nonsense about love and forgiveness for a while, and start dealing with more practical matters – like raising an army and putting together some kind of battle plan…'

'And finding the money,' the companion added.

'And finding the money,' Judas sighed.

'This is dangerous talk,' the companion whispered. Then he leaned forward and whispered more quietly still, so that his whisper sounded almost like a hiss. 'But I think I may have a way to help you.'

'Really?' the disciple whispered back.

'Yes,' the companion continued. 'Some of my employers in the high priest's office would like to have a word with Jesus. Privately. They, too, are concerned about the direction his teaching has taken and feel that if they could just spend some time alone with him, that they might be able to get him back on the right track. If you could lead them to some quiet spot where they could meet with him, I am sure that they would reward you handsomely.'

'How handsomely?' Judas asked.

The companion smiled. 'I keep forgetting that I am dealing with a practical man here, my friend.' And then he paused and then he thought. He had the look of a man bartering for some great treasure. 'What would you say to... oh... thirty pieces of silver?'

Judas' eyes lit up. 'I would say, "You have a deal!" '

The companion stood and reached out his hand.

'So I can count on you?' he asked.

'Of course,' Judas answered. 'At the first opportunity. And the money...?'

'Trust me,' the companion smiled. 'It'll be fine.'

And as he walked away, Judas smiled, as well. Everything was back on course. Plans, programmes, practical matters. And finally the money to make it happen.

'Thirty pieces of silver,' he grinned. 'With that kind of money, I can really make a difference in the world!'

The Magician's Tale

• • • • • • • • • • •

THE STORY OF SIMON MAGUS

Simon was jealous. It was as simple as that. Somebody had something he wanted. Not a possession. Not a position. Not even a person. No, it was power – power to make the lame walk and the blind see.

His jealousy ate at him. And that ugly mix of frustration, disappointment, anger and bitterness blinded him to everything but his own desire. And led him to do something terrible. That's the way it is with jealousy. Sometimes the jealousy itself makes it even harder to get what we want.

The sad thing is that, in time, the very thing that Simon wanted might well have been his for the asking.

But it was not for the grabbing.

It was not for the taking.

And it was certainly not his for the buying.

Whenever Simon walked through the streets of Samaria, people stopped and took notice.

Sometimes they pointed.

Sometimes they bowed.

Sometimes they found the courage to wave hello.

And sometimes they even shouted, 'Look, there goes the Great Power of God!'

Simon loved every minute of it! He didn't show it, of course. It would have spoiled the air of mystery and awe he had worked so hard to create. So he would nod, and stretch forth his hand – ever so slightly – like a king waving to his subjects.

But Simon was no king, nor royalty of any kind, for that matter. No, Simon was a sorcerer. Or, to be more precise, he had quick hands, a way with healing potions, and a knack for making predictions that, more often than not, came true. Magician? Rogue? Call it what you like – Simon's chosen 'occupation' had brought him fame and wealth and power, and, as far as he was concerned, that was all that mattered.

And then, suddenly, one day, everything changed.

Simon walked through the streets of Samaria, and nobody noticed.

Nobody pointed.

Nobody bowed.

Nobody said, 'There goes the Great Power of God!'

For the streets were empty and there was nobody there. Well, almost nobody. A boy ran past Simon, nearly knocking him down along the way.

'What's the hurry?' Simon called.

'It's the miracle man!' the boy shouted back over his shoulder. 'He's in the fields on the edge of town!'

'A miracle man?' Simon grumbled to himself. 'The last thing I need is competition. But what should I do?' he wondered. 'Should I ignore the man completely? Or should I hang about at the edge of the crowd, have a good look at his bag of tricks, and then make him look a fool in front of everyone?'

As Simon pondered this question, someone else rushed by, bumping into him. It was Nathan, the town baker.

'Beg your pardon,' he muttered. 'But... well... at the edge of town...'

'Yes, I know,' said Simon, with a condescending smile. 'A miracle man – or so they say.'

'Oh, he's a miracle man, all right!' the baker answered. 'Blind folk see! Lame folk walk! Come and see for yourself.'

'Yes, I think I'll do just that,' said Simon, the smile dropping from his face.

The baker rushed off again. But Simon took his time. There was a part of him that wanted very much to see this miracle man, and another part that was afraid of seeing him at all.

When Simon finally reached the crowd, no one even noticed him. No one pointed or bowed or waved. For every eye was trained on the man at the front.

'He doesn't look like much of a sorcerer,' Simon thought. 'Those robes are far too plain and his gestures much too awkward.'

Old Hannah, who had walked with a limp for years, stepped forward and held her hands out to the miracle man. And Simon just rolled his eyes.

'Good luck with that one!' he thought. 'A dozen healing potions – and all she can do is complain about the taste!'

The man took hold of Hannah's hands. He bowed his head and shut his eyes and whispered some kind of spell – or at least that's what it looked like to Simon.

'Where's the drama?' Simon wondered. 'Where's the

flair?' And then he grunted, so that everyone around him could hear, 'Not exactly a real magician, if you ask me.' And he turned to walk away.

But at that moment, a cheer burst forth from the crowd!

Simon turned back to look – and there was Hannah, leaping and dancing as if she was nine years old!

'It's amazing!' someone shouted.

'It's a miracle!' shouted someone else.

And then someone at the front shouted something that made Simon cringe.

'This man must be the Great Power of God!'

Now Simon wanted to shout as well. He wanted to shout, 'No! This man is not the Great Power of God! I am!'

But much to his surprise the miracle man said it for him.

'Please don't call me that,' he said. 'I am not the Great Power of God, or any power at all. My name is Philip. I am a follower of Jesus of Nazareth, and it is through his power that this woman has been healed.'

Simon was shocked. If he had made old Hannah walk, he would have raised his arms to the sky and commanded the crowd to fall at his feet. And they would have – he was sure of it! But this man? What was this man up to? What did he want?

'I only want to talk to you,' Philip continued, 'to tell you about this Jesus whom I follow.' And to Simon's amazement, that's exactly what he did. He took no money. He asked no favours. He simply went on healing people, and as he did so, he told them about a man named Jesus.

'Jesus was God's own Son,' Philip explained. Then he laid his hands on a troubled man, who screamed and then smiled gently as if something bad had left him. 'Jesus came to overcome evil. He came so that people could be part of his kingdom – a kingdom of goodness and peace.

'Jesus was a teacher, too.' Philip went on. And as a little girl who had been blind looked for the first time at her mother, Philip said, 'We are all blind, in our own way. Jesus came to help us see more clearly what's important and to show us the truth about God and life and love.'

Simon listened carefully as Philip lowered his voice.

'Sadly,' Philip sighed, 'there were people who did not like Jesus. So they crucified him and buried him in a tomb.'

The crowd sighed along with him and then watched as a smile broke out on his face.

'But God would not let that be the end of the story,' he said with a grin. 'So, three days later, he raised Jesus from the dead! I know people who saw him. And now that he has gone back to be with his Father in heaven, he wants all of us to follow him and be part of his kingdom of love!'

Simon watched as the people streamed towards Philip. He was having trouble making sense of any of this. But there was one thing he knew for certain – there was no way that his own power could even begin to compare with the power of this Philip, or the Jesus he spoke of. And if he couldn't beat them, then there was only one choice left. He would have to join them, and get hold of this power for himself.

Several days went by, and Simon stayed as close to Philip as he possibly could. He listened closely to Philip's prayers (they were definitely not spells, Philip had explained politely). He carefully watched Philip's movements. But, try as he might, Simon could not make the power of Jesus work for him.

Simon was disappointed. Simon was frustrated. And it didn't help that everyone's attention was still focused on Philip. That is, until two of Philip's friends came to town.

'The older one is Peter,' Philip explained to Simon. 'And the younger one is John. Both of these men were Jesus' disciples. They lived and worked with him for three years. They saw him when he rose from the dead. And now they have come here from Jerusalem to pray for all the new believers.'

Simon watched these two men, and as far as he could tell, they didn't look any more special than Philip. 'Why,' Simon thought, 'the older one looks just like a common labourer or fisherman!'

Philip, however, treated them with the utmost respect. And as soon as they began praying and placing their hands on the believers, Simon understood why. For the most amazing things began to happen.

Some people fainted dead away. Some began speaking in other languages. And others just leaped up and down for joy.

Simon listened carefully, and he heard the two men say the exact same words, 'May the Lord fill you with his Holy Spirit.'

'Aha!' Simon thought. 'That's the secret. The power lies in this Holy Spirit.' And as soon as he got the chance, he took Peter and John aside. He'd had a good look at them. Maybe Philip hadn't wanted any money, but these men (the older one in particular) looked as if they could use a set of new clothes. And so he bowed and said, as humbly as he could, 'I, too, would like to have the power to pass on this Holy Spirit. How much would it cost to buy it from you?'

Peter looked at John. John looked at Peter. And Simon thought, for a moment that they might ask for time to talk together about the price. But when Peter gave his answer, Simon realized that he had got it all wrong, again!

'A curse on you and your money!' Peter shouted. And Simon shrank back at the force of his words. 'The Holy Spirit is God's free gift!' Peter went on. 'And to offer to buy it with money shows that your heart is not right with God at all. I can see you are full of bitterness and jealousy. And the best thing you can do is ask God's forgiveness for what you have done!'

If Simon had thought about it, for even a minute, he would have seen that Peter was right. Bitterness – at losing his fame and power and attention – had been driving him all along. But Simon had only heard the curse. And he thought that someone powerful enough to bless the blind and the lame could make his curses come true as well. So he begged Peter to remove the curse and then hurried away from the crowd.

No one knows for certain what happened to Simon. But there is an old story which suggests that his bitterness never did go away. The story says that Simon took his bag of tricks to other places in the ancient world, and that he managed to rebuild his reputation. But then one day, many years later, he ran into Peter again. Still angry over his embarrassment in Samaria, he challenged Peter to a contest.

'You say that this Jesus was buried in the earth for three days and then rose again. To prove that I am even greater than he, I will be buried, as well. And I, too, shall rise in three days.'

That's what Simon did, so the story goes. He had himself buried in the ground. And as far as anyone knows, he's buried there still!

The Fanatic's Tale

● ● ● ● ● ● ● ● ● ● ● ●

THE STORY OF PAUL

Sometimes people do the wrong things for the wrong reason. They steal because they are greedy. They lie because they don't want to get caught. They cheat because they are too lazy to do their own work.

But there is another reason that people sometimes do what is wrong. The right reason. So they think anyway.

Saul was one of those people. He wanted to please God, and serve God, and live his life for God. But he found himself threatening and torturing and even killing, all in the name of God. All for the 'right' reason. The problem was that Saul misunderstood God, as so many do when they use force or violence to try to do God's will. When Saul finally 'met' God, he realized how wrong he had been. He saw a God working not through brutal force but through kindness and love, mercy and forgiveness.

He took the garments, one by one, and hung them over his arm. Shoulder to shoulder, he folded them. Crease to crease. Sleeve to sleeve. Each one neat. Each one straight. Each one perfect.

Saul knew that his was a small contribution. But on the road to perfection, every detail mattered. And even the tiniest step in the wrong direction could send one wandering off the path for ever.

No further proof was needed than the man on the ground before him. Saul had listened carefully to Stephen's speech. The man knew the scriptures well. From Abraham to Moses, from Joshua to David, he had rehearsed the history of Israel with passion and poise. Every point was well argued, every detail well described. But then there was the mis-step. He raised his voice. He pointed his finger. And finally Stephen accused the council of murdering the long-awaited Messiah!

How could Stephen have been so foolish? How could he have wandered so far from the truth? 'Stiff-necked', that's what he had called the council—'murderers'! And over what? The death of a blasphemous carpenter from Galilee, who had gone against everything that Saul believed by teaching that he was more important than Moses or the Temple or God's own Law.

Jesus had deserved to die. The Law of God demanded it. And this man – this Stephen – deserved no less.

The rocks were crashing down upon him, even now – cracking his head and his limbs, crushing the life out of him. And his sweaty executioners would soon want their robes back. So Saul stood and held their garments and watched Stephen calling out his blasphemy, 'Receive my spirit, Lord Jesus!' (as if this Jesus were God himself!) until he breathed his last.

'Jesus!' Saul soon came to hate that name. Stephen's death did nothing to slow the spread of that blasphemer's teachings, and Saul was convinced that something needed to be done. He knew that false teaching could be as strong as the truth. And this particular teaching was like a cancer – popping up here and there, all over Judea – infecting one community after another.

It had to be stopped. And Saul knew that he was the man to do it.

He had the background – a long and noble family tradition.

He had the education – there was no finer teacher than his master, the Pharisee Gamaliel.

And most of all, he had the discipline. 'A Pharisee's Pharisee' – that's what someone had called him once. And he had taken it as a compliment. Yes, he'd heard the whispers about some of the teachers – 'those Pharisees are proud, they're holier-than-thou.' But he had always assumed that was nothing more than jealousy. Right beliefs. Right actions. That's what God demanded. And surely every community needed individuals who were willing to sacrifice everything so that everyone could see what believing the right thing and doing the right thing would look like if it were lived out day by day.

Saul was such an individual. And he was convinced that only a person like him – dedicated to observing the tiniest details of the Law – could stand against the spread of this false teaching. This was the job he'd been born for. Now he could show, once and for all, his absolute devotion to God.

And so Saul set to work. Some of Jesus' followers he arrested and sent to jail. Others he threatened with violence. Still others he beat. And some he even put to death!

It was hard work. It was tiring. And it was far from pleasant. Torture and threats and death brought Saul no joy. In fact, there were times when the whole thing nearly broke his heart. The followers of Jesus were devoted people – passionate about their faith. In different circumstances, he might have called them his brothers and sisters.

But they were wrong! What they believed was wrong! They had taken a mere man and set him up beside God himself! And God would not stand for that. Such arrogance, such sin, would have to be punished. That is what the Law said. That is how God worked. And there was no way around it.

And so Saul went on – the instrument of God's punishment. And his efficiency and attention to detail soon made him the man most feared by the followers of Jesus. In spite of his hard work, however, the heresy continued to spread. And when word reached him that it had even travelled up north to Damascus, he went straight to the high priest and asked for permission to seek out the blasphemers and bring them to Jerusalem to face trial.

It was a long trip to Damascus – a hundred miles or so. And Saul was looking forward to the journey's end. Partly because he was tired. And partly because he could not wait to get to work. But as the noonday sun shone down upon his head, he noticed that it was brighter than he had ever seen it before. And then suddenly the light burned brighter still and shone so piercing and white that Saul shut his eyes and fell frightened to the ground.

Words came next – ringing in his ears and banging in his skull.

'Saul! Saul!' the voice pleaded. 'Why do you persecute me, Saul?'

Saul blinked, struggling to understand. 'Persecute?' he thought. 'Surely this voice, this voice from heaven, can't mean me. I teach people and guide them. I am a defender of the One True God!'

And so Saul asked, 'Who are you, Lord?' And the voice answered plainly with the last name Saul expected to hear.

'Jesus,' the voice said. 'I am Jesus. And you are my persecutor.'

On his knees, on the ground, all Saul could think of was Stephen – that other man on his knees, that other man on the ground, with the robes of his executioners in Saul's hands. What had Stephen said before he died? Whom had he called out to? The same voice, the same name, the same light that now blinded Saul. And it was at that moment that Saul's life – like a garment that was ironed and straight and perfect, down to the smallest detail – began to unravel and unfold.

Stephen was not the blasphemer. Stephen was not the one who had got it all wrong. It was Saul, himself, who had wandered off God's path – Saul, God's defender, who had been persecuting God's Messiah all along!

How could he have been so foolish? How could he have been so wrong? Saul folded himself into a bundle – a crumpled pile of sadness and shame. And as the voice commanded him to go to Damascus and wait, his companions pulled him, shaking, to his feet, and discovered that he could no longer see.

It didn't matter to Saul, not really. In spite of his efforts, his very best efforts – his hard work and his sacrifices and his attention to detail – he had still, somehow, managed to do the very opposite of what God wanted. Blindness was the least he deserved.

Blindness, in fact, was almost a kind of refuge. For it kept him from having to face those companions who had looked to him as their model.

For one day, he fasted. No food and no drink. And the enormity of his failure overwhelmed him.

For a second day, he fasted. And the failure was followed by fear and despair.

For a third day, he fasted, and prayed the whole day for God's mercy, convinced, all the while, that his sin would result in one thing only – God's anger. And God's punishment.

And then there came another vision. It started with a visitor and a knock at the door. The visitor's name was Ananias. He was a follower of Jesus. And when he spoke, his voice shook, but Saul could not tell whether it was from anger or from fear.

Saul expected the worst. It was what he deserved. And when his companions protested that he should have nothing to do with this man, Saul shooed them away and quietly asked Ananias to stay.

The vision went on, as Ananias walked slowly towards Saul. And when Ananias' hands landed on Saul's shoulders, both men trembled.

'This is it,' thought Saul. 'I have murdered this man's brothers and sisters. I have beaten them and dragged them off to prison. Wrongly, wrongly have I acted, and now I must face God's punishment.'

'Brother Saul,' Ananias began. And Saul could hardly believe his ears.

'Brother? Brother?!'

'It was the Lord Jesus you saw on the road,' Ananias continued, 'and it was the same Lord Jesus who sent me here to speak with you. He wants you to see again.' The vision ended, and it wasn't long before a real knock came at the front door. It was the same man – Ananias – and, step by step, the dream played itself out before him, until Ananias laid his hands on Saul's shoulders – and he could see!

Saul looked for the first time into Ananias' eyes, and he watched his mouth speak the words he'd only dreamed of hearing.

'It was God himself who did this,' Ananias explained. 'The God of our fathers, Abraham, Isaac and Jacob. He has chosen you, Saul. Chosen you to see the risen Lord, chosen you to hear his voice, and chosen you to tell the whole world of his love and his mercy. So taste his mercy yourself, Saul. Get up. Be baptized. Call upon his name and let him wash away your sins.'

The water felt good. Up over his knees and his waist it flowed. Up further past his chest and face. He was buried beneath the water. And when he rose up again and gasped for his first breath, he knew that he had left something behind in that water for ever. The old Saul was down there, the Saul who'd believed that he could somehow earn God's approval by his efforts, his good works, his attention to detail. The Saul who had almost let his proud devotion to God blind him to the most important thing of all – God's mercy and forgiveness.

And so he came up out of that water a new man. With a new mission. And soon he would have a new name. He would be Paul now, not Saul. And his life would be devoted to helping others find God's mercy and forgiveness, as well.

The Liars' Tale

● ● ● ● ● ● ● ● ● ● ● ● ●

THE STORY OF
ANANIAS AND SAPPHIRA

*Some say that lying is no big deal. 'Everybody does it!' they
suggest. And sadly, even government leaders sometimes try
to convince people that certain lies are all right so that they
keep their positions of power.*

*The interesting thing is that those kinds of excuses usually
come from the people who do the lying. People who get lied to
often have a different opinion. They feel disappointed, angry,
betrayed, and they sometimes have difficulty trusting people
again.*

*Lying hurts. And if you have ever been lied to, you know
exactly what I mean. That's because lying is mostly rooted in
selfishness. We do it to protect ourselves or – as you will see in
the following story – to impress somebody else.*

Yes, everybody does it. But lying is still wrong. And it's definitely a big deal. As a man named Ananias (not the Ananias who befriended Paul!) and his wife, Sapphira, came to discover...

'So what did you think of the sermon, dear?' Ananias asked his wife, Sapphira as they walked along to their friends' house.

'Very... interesting,' she answered, choosing the word carefully. 'And you?'

'A little long-winded, I thought,' said Ananias. 'Nothing against Peter, of course. He's a capable speaker, on the whole, but... well...'

'I know just what you mean,' his wife responded. 'The lack of education shows. We've all noticed it. Why, some of the ladies and I were talking about it just the other day. But he has other qualities.'

'That's just what I was going to say,' agreed Ananias. 'Enthusiasm, passion...'

'And punctuality!' Sapphira added. 'I think that's very important in a church leader.'

Ananias chuckled. 'Yes, well, you should know, dear.'

'No one's perfect,' Sapphira frowned. 'And besides, I'm getting better. I'm not nearly as late for things as I used to be.'

Ananias glanced at the sun. 'Well, here's your chance to prove it,' he said. 'If we don't hurry, we're going to be late for dinner with the Bar-Josephs!'

Sapphira frowned again and slowed her pace. 'But they're so... intense!' she moaned. 'With their "Hallelujah!" this, and their "Praise the Lord!" that.'

'Levi and Hannah Bar-Joseph are important members of

the church,' Ananias explained. 'Second cousins to the apostle Bartholomew! So if we want to get ahead in the church then we have to get on with them.'

'But the "Hallelujahs"!' Sapphira countered.

'Just hold your tongue and smile,' Ananias ordered. 'Now hurry!'

Dinner at the Bar-Josephs was exceptional. But, as they feared, Ananias and Sapphira found the conversation much more difficult to swallow.

'I was truly blessed by the sermon today!' said Hannah Bar-Joseph enthusiastically.

'Hallelujah!' added her husband, Levi.

'Why, I could listen to Peter all day long!' she went on.

'Praise the Lord!' Levi shouted.

'God is going to use that man in a powerful way!' she concluded.

And Levi managed to squeeze in one more 'Hallelujah' before his 'Amen'.

Ananias glanced at Sapphira. He could see the corners of her mouth start to quiver. So he quickly changed the subject.

'There were a lot of new people at worship today,' he noted.

'More every week!' Hannah smiled.

But before her husband could add yet another 'Hallelujah', Sapphira spoke up. 'Don't you think we have to be the tiniest bit careful, though?' she asked. 'All these new people, I mean. There were a few sitting behind me, today. Nothing but rags on. And their children – sniffling and coughing and making all kinds of noise. Why, I could hardly hear Peter's excellent sermon. They're just not the sort... well, you know what I'm saying.'

A silence descended on the room. Ananias noted the

shocked expressions on the faces of his hosts. If he had been sitting next to his wife, he would have nudged her, or poked her, or even given her a quick kick on the shins. But that was out of the question, so hastily he jumped back into the conversation.

'What my wife means to say is that there are so many of these poor souls for us to care for.' Then Ananias hesitated, weighing his words carefully. 'And care for them, we must… as Jesus would… care for them,' he added finally.

Hannah looked at Levi.

Levi looked at Hannah.

And then, together, both of them shouted, 'Hallelujah!'

And Ananias breathed a quiet sigh of relief.

'Oh, but you know there is a way we can care for these poor souls,' said Hannah. 'I'm sure you've heard. Everyone is selling their things. Jewellery, clothing, even houses and land. Why, just today, I heard that Barnabas, that sweet man, sold a very nice piece of property. And all that money will go into a common fund to meet the needs of just the kinds of folk that you described.'

Ananias looked at Sapphira.

Sapphira fingered the shiny bracelet round her wrist.

Neither of them had ever heard of such a thing. Both of them were horrified at the thought. But admitting that to the Bar-Josephs was simply not an option. So Ananias just smiled and said, 'What a splendid idea!'

'Yes, how inventive,' added Sapphira, slowly slipping the bracelet up under the end of her sleeve.

'To be honest,' said Levi, 'that is one of the reasons we invited you to dinner today. We understand that you own a field or two out in the country and wondered if you might part with one of them and give the money to help these poor people?'

Another silence descended on the group, and this time it was Ananias and Sapphira who looked nervously at each other.

Ananias cleared his throat. 'Well, that would certainly be something to think about,' he said slowly.

'Yes, to *think* about,' said Sapphira, more deliberately. 'On our way *home*,' she added, hoping that, in his present state of shock, Ananias would still be able to catch the hint.

'Home. Yes,' repeated Ananias. 'It's about time, isn't it? Lovely meal. Thanks very much. And we'll let you know – um...'

'At the next gathering?' suggested Hannah.

'All right then,' Ananias smiled weakly.

'Amen to that!' shouted Levi.

And Ananias and Sapphira staggered out of the door for home.

'Well, *I've* thought about it,' grunted Sapphira, when they were no more than a minute's walk down the road. 'And I think it's the stupidest thing I've ever heard!'

'What?' Ananias grunted back. 'More stupid than insulting the poor and needy in front of holy Hannah back there? If you hadn't opened your mouth, we wouldn't be in this mess at all!'

'Oh, really?' Sapphira snapped back. 'You heard them – that's why they invited us! "They're important!" you said. "We have to get on with them," you said. Well look where it's got us! More noisy children! More stinking beggars! More ruined worship! And we have to pay for it!!'

'That's enough!' snapped Ananias. 'There's a way out of this.' Then he stopped. Then he smiled. 'And I may have just thought of it!'

'Well, hallelujah!' Sapphira sneered.

But Ananias ignored her and went on. 'Nobody really knows what our land is worth, do they?'

'Well, I should hope *you* know!' Sapphira grunted.

'Of course I know,' sighed Ananias. 'The point is that no one else knows! So why don't we simply sell the land for what it's worth, keep half for ourselves and give away the other half?'

Sapphira's eyes lit up. 'That's brilliant!' she said. 'We keep part of what really belongs to us, anyway, and we still manage to impress Hannah and Levi and all the rest!'

Ananias paused. 'My only real concern is Peter. We're going to have to lie to him, after all. I hope he doesn't catch on.'

Sapphira smiled and tapped the side of her head. 'He's not too bright, remember? We've got nothing to worry about there. And besides, it's not really lying. We'll say something like, "Here's what we got for the land." And then it's all down to what the meaning of the word "got" is, isn't it?'

Sapphira shook her bracelet out from under her sleeve. She took her husband's hand. And they walked home together happily.

The next Sunday, Sapphira was late, as usual. Late getting up. Late dressing. Late for breakfast. And so, Ananias left without her, as he always did.

'Just remember to keep the story straight!' he shouted, as he stormed out of the door. 'And thanks for going out of your way to be so supportive!'

Sapphira grinned. Being late today was more than just a bad habit. She was a lousy liar and she knew it. So why not let Ananias do the 'dirty work' and show up later for all the praise!

Ananias was sweating by the time he got to the meeting place.

'There's no reason to be nervous,' he assured himself. And he smiled and waved at the Bar-Josephs and held up his money bag. 'The deal was done very quietly,' he thought. 'The buyer lives in another town. There's no way that anyone could know.'

So he sang the psalms and listened to the sermon and then rose to join the queue with the others who had sold their belongings.

Ananias waited impatiently, wiping the sweat from his forehead and wishing this was over. He watched the others, he worked up his nerve, and he consoled himself with thoughts of how impressed everyone would be. Finally, it was his turn.

This was the first time that Ananias had been so close to Peter. He was surprised by the man's height. And even more surprised by the look in his eye. Sapphira was wrong. This man was no fool. And Ananias was not comforted by that thought – not at all.

'I… that is, we… my wife and I,' Ananias stammered, 'we sold a piece of land. And here is the money we got for it.'

Peter looked at Ananias, deep into his eyes. A drop of sweat fell from Ananias' forehead and rolled down one cheek.

'Is this *all* the money you received for the land?' Peter asked.

'Oh, yes!' Ananias lied. 'All of it. You can ask my wife!' He looked around, nervously, for Sapphira. What was keeping her? Peter's voice snapped him back to attention.

'I do not need to ask your wife,' said Peter solemnly. 'The Holy Spirit has already told me that what you say is a lie.'

Ananias swallowed hard. Everyone had gone quiet. And all he could hear was Peter's voice and the excited drumming of his own heart.

'Why did you do this wicked thing?' asked Peter. 'The land was yours. No one forced you to sell it. And after you did, you were free to split up the money any way you liked. So why have you lied to us? And worse still, why have you lied to God?'

Ananias looked round the room. And as he looked, his heart beat faster and faster still. Some faces were confused. Some were angry. But nobody was impressed. Nobody. And then Ananias's heart stopped beating altogether. And he fell to the ground, dead.

Sapphira, meanwhile, had no idea what had happened, no clue that their plan had failed, or that her husband had died. She was still determined to give Ananias plenty of time to work things out. So she fussed with her hair. And ate a meal. And stopped at her neighbour's house for a long gossip. In fact, three hours had passed by the time she got to the meeting place.

Everyone was still there – talking or praying or having a bite to eat. But when Sapphira entered the room, everything went quiet.

'They were obviously more impressed than we imagined!' she thought. But when Sapphira looked more closely at the faces in the room, she realized she was mistaken.

'Sapphira,' Peter called, 'I'd like a word with you.'

This was not looking good. For a moment Sapphira thought about walking out and going back home. But what would Ananias say? And where was her husband, anyway?

'Ananias told us that you sold a piece of land,' Peter explained.

'That's right,' answered Sapphira as confidently as she could.

'And he told us that the land sold for this much.' Here Peter held up the money bag. 'And that you were giving it all to help the poor.'

Sapphira decided to play it cool. 'Well, that's his money bag,' she chuckled. 'And if that's what he told you, then that must be the case!'

Sapphira looked around. No one was chuckling with her.

Peter just shook his head. 'So you were in this together? Now both of you have lied to God.'

'No, no, no!' Sapphira smiled and tried to explain. 'Not lying. You see, it all depends how you look at it. It all depends on the meaning of the word "got"...'

But before she could finish, Peter spoke again. 'Listen, Sapphira, and listen well. The feet of the men who buried your husband are outside the door. Those men will bury you as well.'

Bury? Husband? Sapphira wondered. But before she could think another thought, she dropped dead to the ground, just like Ananias.

The people certainly were impressed. There was tremendous fear, for a start. And Ananias and Sapphira were the talk of the town for years. Something Sapphira had always wanted.

But what Ananias and Sapphira were remembered for wasn't quite what they'd had in mind!

Also by Bob Hartman

ANGELS, ANGELS ALL AROUND

Have you ever wondered what an angel looks like? Do all angels look the same? What if God created angels with all the wonderful variety of the birds of the air and the fish in the sea? What if every angel is unique – each one as different as you are from anyone else?

Professional storyteller BOB HARTMAN takes an imaginative look at ten Bible stories, including the men in the Fiery Furnace, Daniel in the Lions' Den and the Christmas story. His tales will leave you wondering – are there really angels all around?